THE WAY TO WEALTH

THE WAY TO WEALTH

ADVICE, HINTS, AND TIPS
ON BUSINESS, MONEY, AND FINANCE

BENJAMIN FRANKLIN

Skyhorse Publishing

Skyhorse Publishing books may be purchased in bulk at special discounts for sales promotion, corporate gifts, fund-raising, or educational purposes. Special editions can also be created to specifications. For details, contact the Special Sales Department, Skyhorse Publishing, 307 West 36th Street, 11th Floor, New York, NY 10018 or info@skyhorsepublishing.com.

www.skyhorsepublishing.com

10 9 8 7 6 5 4 3 2 1

Library of Congress Cataloging-in-Publication Data

Franklin, Benjamin, 1706-1790.
 The way to wealth : advice, hints, and tips on business, money, and finance / Benjamin Franklin.
    p. cm.
 ISBN 978-1-61608-201-7 (alk. paper)
 1. Finance, Personal. 2. Saving and investment. 3. Maxims, American. 4. Franklin, Benjamin, 1706-1790--Miscellanea. I. Title.
 HG179.F715 2011
 332.024'01--dc22

                        2010036197

Printed in the United States of America

Industry, Perseverance, & Frugality,
make Fortune yield.

CONTENTS

The Way to Wealth 1

The Whistle 14

Necessary Hints to Those That Would Be Rich 18

The Way to Make Money Plenty in Every Man's Pocket 21

Advice to a Young Tradesman 24

On Luxury, Idleness, and Industry 28

On Smuggling, and its Various Species 36

On Truth and Falsehood 43

On the Usefulness of Mathematics 49

On the Price of Corn, and the Management of the Poor 55

An Economical Project 62

Plan for Saving One Hundred Thousand Pounds 71

A Modest Enquiry into the Nature and Necessity of
    a Paper Currency 74

Letters to Mrs. Jane Mecom 102

Letter to Miss Stevenson, Wanstead 109

Letter to Dr. Priestly 112

Letter to Benjamin Vaughan 115

Letter from Anthony Afterwit 118

Notes 124

THE WAY TO WEALTH

As clearly shown in the practice of an old Pennsylvania Almanac, entitled, "Poor Richard Improved."

Courteous Reader,

I have heard that nothing gives an author so great pleasure as to find his works respectfully quoted by others. Judge, then, how much I must have been gratified by an incident I am going to relate to you. I stopped my horse lately where a great number of people were collected at an auction of merchants' goods. The hour of the sale not being come, they were conversing on the badness of the times; and one of the company called to a plain, clean old man, with white locks, "Pray, Father Abraham, what think you of the times? Will not these heavy taxes quite ruin the country? How shall we ever be able to pay them? What would you advise us to do?" Father Abraham stood up and replied, "If you would have my advice, I will give it you in short; 'for a word to the wise is enough,' as Poor Richard says." They joined in desiring him to speak his mind; and, gathering round him, he proceeded as follows:

"Friends,' said he, 'the taxes are indeed very heavy, and if those laid on by the government were the only ones we had to pay, we might more easily discharge them; but we have many others, and much more grievous to some of us. We are taxed twice as much by our idleness, three times as much by our pride, and four times as much by our folly; and from these taxes the commissioners cannot ease or deliver us, by allowing an abatement. However, let us hearken to good advice, and something may be done for us: 'God helps them that help themselves,' as Poor Richard says.

I. "It would be thought a hard government that should tax its people one tenth part of their time, to be employed in its service; but idleness taxes many of us much more; sloth, by bringing on diseases, absolutely shortens life. 'Sloth, like rust, consumes faster than labour wears; while the used key is always bright,' as Poor Richard says. 'But dost thou love life, then do not squander time, for that is the stuff life is made of,' as Poor Richard says. How much more than is necessary do we spend in sleep, forgetting that 'the sleeping fox catches no poultry, and that, 'there will be sleeping enough in the grave,' as Poor Richard says.

" 'If time be of all things the most precious, wasting time must be,' as Poor Richard says, 'the greatest prodigality'; since, as he elsewhere tells us, 'Lost time is never found again; and what we call time enough, always proves little enough'. Let us, then, up and be doing, and doing to the purpose; so by diligence shall we do more with less perplexity. 'Sloth makes all things difficult, but industry all easy, and He that riseth late must trot all day, and shall scarce overtake his business at night; while Laziness travels so slowly, that Poverty soon overtakes him. Drive thy business, let not that drive thee; and Early to bed and early to rise, makes a man healthy, wealthy, and wise,' as Poor Richard says.

"So what signifies wishing and hoping for better times? We may make these times better if we bestir ourselves. 'Industry need not wish, and he that lives upon hopes will die fasting. There are no gains without pains; then help, hands, for I have no lands,' or, if I have, they are smartly taxed. 'He that hath a trade hath an estate; and he that hath a calling hath an office of profit and honor,' as Poor Richard says; but then the trade must be worked at, and the calling followed, or neither the estate nor the office will enable us to pay our taxes. If we are industrious, we shall never starve; for, 'at the workingman's house hunger looks in, but dares not enter.' Nor will the bailiff or the constable enter; for 'Industry pays debts, while despair increaseth them.' What though you have found no treasure, nor has any rich relation left you a legacy? 'Diligence is the mother of luck, and God gives all things to industry. Then plough deep while sluggards sleep, and you shall have corn to sell and to keep.' Work while it is called today, for you know not how much you may be hindered to-morrow. 'One today is worth two tomorrows,' as Poor Richard says; and farther, 'Never leave that till tomorrow which you can do today.' If you were a servant, would you not be ashamed that a good master should catch you idle? Are you, then, your own master? Be ashamed to catch yourself idle when there is so much to be done for yourself, your family, and your country. Handle your tools without mittens; remember that 'The cat in gloves catches no mice,' as Poor Richard says. It is true there is much to be done, and perhaps you are weak-handed; but stick to it steadily, and you will see great effects; for 'Constant dropping wears away stones; and by diligence and patience the mouse ate in two the cable; and little strokes fell great oaks.'

"Methinks I hear some of you say, 'Must a man afford himself no leisure?' I will tell thee, my friend, what Poor Richard says: 'Employ thy time well, if thou meanest to gain leisure; and, since thou art not sure of a minute, throw not away an hour.' Leisure is time for doing something useful; this leisure the diligent man will obtain, but the lazy man never; for 'A life of leisure and a life of laziness are two things. Many, without labour, would live by their wits only, but they break for want of stock;' whereas industry gives comfort, and plenty, and respect. 'Fly pleasures, and they will follow you. The diligent spinner has a large shift; and now I have a sheep and a cow, everybody bids me good morrow.'

II. "But with our industry we must likewise be steady, settled, and careful, and oversee our own affairs with our own eyes, and not trust too much to others; for, as Poor Richard says,

> 'I never saw an oft-removed tree,
> Nor yet an oft-removed family.
> That throve so well as those that settled be.'

And again, 'Three removes are as bad as a fire'; and again, 'Keep thy shop, and thy shop will keep thee'; and again,

'If you would have your business done, go; if not, send.'
And again, 'He that by the plough would thrive, himself
must either hold or drive.'

And again, 'The eye of a master will do more work than
both his hands'; and again, 'Want of care does us more
damage than want of knowledge'; and again, 'Not to oversee workmen is to leave them your purse open.' Trusting
too much to others' care is the ruin of many; for, 'In the
affairs of this world men are saved, not by faith, but by
the want of it'; but a man's own care is profitable; for, 'If
you would have a faithful servant, and one that you like,
serve yourself. A little neglect may breed great mischief;
for want of a nail the shoe was lost; for want of a shoe the
horse was lost; and for want of a horse the rider was lost',
being overtaken and slain by the enemy; all for the want of
care about a horseshoe nail.

III. "So much for industry, my friends, and attention to
one's own business; but to these we must add frugality, if
we would make our industry more certainly successful. A
man may, if he knows not how to save as he gets, 'keep his
nose all his life to the grindstone, and die not worth a groat
at last. A fat kitchen makes a lean will'; and

> 'Many estates are spent in the getting,
> Since women for tea forsook spinning, and knitting,
> And men for punch forsook hewing and splitting.'

'If you would be wealthy, think of saving as well as of getting. The Indies have not made Spain rich, because her outgoes are greater than her incomes.'

"Away, then, with your expensive follies, and you will not then have so much cause to complain of hard times, heavy taxes, and chargeable families; for 'Women and wine, game and deceit, make the wealth small, and the want great.'

"And farther, 'What maintains one vice would bring up two children.' You may think, perhaps, that a little tea, or a little punch now and then, diet a little more costly, clothes a little finer, and a little entertainment now and then, can be no great matter; but remember, 'Many a little makes a mickle.' Beware of little expenses; 'A small leak will sink a great ship,' as Poor Richard says; and again, 'Who dainties love, shall beggars prove'; and moreover, 'Fools make feasts, and wise men eat them.' Here you are all got together at this sale of fineries and knickknacks. You call them goods; but, if you do not take care, they will prove evils to some of you. You expect they will be sold cheap, and perhaps they may for less than they cost; but, if you have no occasion for them, they must be dear to you. Remember what Poor Richard says: 'buy what thou hast no need of, and ere long thou shall tell thy necessaries.' And again, 'At a great pennyworth pause a while.' He means, that perhaps the cheapness is apparent only, and not real; or the bargain, by straitening thee in thy business, may do thee more harm than good. For in another place he says, 'Many have been ruined by buying good pennyworths.' Again, 'It is foolish to lay out money in a purchase of repentance'; and yet this folly is practised every day at auctions, for want of minding the Almanac. Many a one, for the sake of finery on the back, have gone with a hungry belly, and half starved their families. 'Silks and satins, scarlet and velvets, put out the kitchen fire,' as Poor Richard says. These are not the necessaries of life; they can scarcely be called the conveniences; and yet, only because they look pretty, how many want to have them! By these and other extravagances, the genteel are reduced to poverty, and forced to borrow of those whom they formerly despised, but who, through industry and frugality, have maintained their standing; in which case it appears plainly that 'a ploughman on his legs is higher than a gentleman on his knees,' as Poor Richard says. Perhaps they have had a small estate left them, which they knew not the getting of; they think 'it is day, and will never be night'; that a little to be spent out of so much is not worth minding; but 'Always taking out of the mealtub and never putting in, soon comes to the bottom,' as Poor Richard says; and then, 'When the well is dry, they know the worth of water.' But this they might have known before if they had taken his advice. 'If you would know the value of money, go and try to borrow some; for he that goes a borrowing goes a sorrowing,' as Poor Richard says; and indeed so does he that lends to such people, when he goes to get it in again. Poor Dick farther advises, and says, 'Fond pride of dress is sure a very curse; Ere fancy you consult, consult your purse.'

"And again, 'pride is as loud a beggar as want, and a great deal more saucy.' When you have bought one fine thing, you must buy ten more, that your appearance may be all of a piece; but Poor Dick says, 'it is easier to suppress the first desire than to satisfy all that follow it.' And it is as truly folly for the poor to ape the rich, as for the frog to swell in order to equal the ox. 'Vessels large may venture more, But little boats should keep near shore.'

"It is, however, a folly soon punished; for, as Poor Richard says, 'pride that dines on vanity, sups on contempt. Pride breakfasted with plenty, dined with poverty, and supped with infamy.' And, after all, of what use is this pride of appearance, for which so much is risked, so much is suffered? It cannot promote health nor ease pain; it makes no increase of merit in the person; it creates envy; it hastens misfortune.

"But what madness must it be to run in debt for these superfluities? We are offered, by the terms of this sale, six months' credit; and that, perhaps, has induced some of us to attend it, because we cannot spare the ready money, and hope now to be fine without it. But ah! think what you do when you run in debt; you give to another power over your liberty. If you cannot pay at the time, you will be ashamed to see your creditor; you will be in fear when you speak to him; you will make poor, pitiful, sneaking excuses, and, by degrees, come to lose your veracity, and sink into base, downright lying; for 'The second vice is lying, the first is running in debt,' as Poor Richard says; and again, to the same purpose, 'lying rides upon debt's back,' whereas a freeborn ought not to be ashamed nor afraid to see or speak to any man living. But poverty often deprives a man of all spirit and virtue. 'It is hard for an empty bag to stand upright.' What would you think of that prince or of that government who should issue an edict forbidding you to dress like a gentleman or gentlewoman, on pain of imprisonment or servitude? Would you not say that you were free, have a right to dress as you please, and that such an edict would be a breach of your privileges, and such a government tyrannical? And yet you are about to put your self under such tyranny, when you run in debt for such dress! Your creditor has authority, at his pleasure, to deprive you of your liberty, by confining you in jail till you shall be able to pay him. When you have got your bargain, you may, perhaps, think little of payment; but, as Poor Richard says, 'Creditors have better memories than debtors; creditors are a superstitious sect, great observers of set days and times.' The day comes round before you are aware, and the demand is made before you are prepared to satisfy it; or, if you bear your debt in mind, the term, which at first seemed so long, will, as it lessens, appear extremely short. Time will seem to have added wings to his heels as well as his shoulders. 'Those have a short Lent who owe money to be paid at Easter.' At present, perhaps, you may think yourselves in thriving circumstances, and that you can bear a little extravagance without injury; but 'For age and want save while you may; No morning sun lasts a whole day.'

"Gain may be temporary and uncertain, but ever, while you live, expense is constant and certain; and 'It is easier to build two chimneys than to keep one in fuel,' as Poor Richard says; so, 'Rather go to bed supperless than rise in debt.' 'Get what you can, and what you get hold, 'Tis the stone that will turn all your lead into gold.'

IV. "This doctrine, my friends, is reason and wisdom; but, after all, do not depend too much upon your own industry, and frugality, and prudence, though excellent things; for they may all be blasted, without the blessing of Heaven; and, therefore, ask that blessing humbly, and be not uncharitable to those that at present seem to want it, but comfort and help them. Remember, Job suffered, and was afterward prosperous.

"And now, to conclude, 'experience keeps a dear school, but fools will learn in no other,' as Poor Richard says, and scarce in that; for it is true, 'we may give advice, but we cannot give conduct.' However, remember this, 'they that will not be counselled cannot be helped'; and farther, that, 'if you will not hear Reason, she will surely rap your knuckles,' as Poor Richard says."

Thus the old gentleman ended his harangue. The people heard it, and approved the doctrine; and immediately practised the contrary, just as if it had been a common sermon; for the auction opened, and they began to buy extravagantly. I found the good man had thoroughly studied my Almanacs, and digested all I had dropped on these topics during the course of twenty-five years. The frequent mention he made of me must have tired any one else; but my vanity was wonderfully delighted with it, though I was conscious that not a tenth part of the wisdom was my own which he ascribed to me, but rather the gleanings that I had made of the sense of all ages and nations. However, I resolved to be the better for the echo of it; and, though I had at first determined to buy stuff for a new coat, I went away resolved to wear my old one a little longer. Reader,

if thou wilt do the same, thy profit will be as great as mine.
I am, as ever, thine to serve thee,

Richard Saunders

If you'd know the value of money,
go and borrow some.

Great spenders are bad lenders.

THE WHISTLE

Passy, November 10, 1779

To Madame Brillon,

I am charmed with your description of Paradise, and with your plan of living there; and I approve much of your conclusion, that, in the meantime, we should draw all the good we can from this world. In my opinion, we might all draw more good from it than we do, and suffer less evil, if we would take care not to give too much for whistles. For to me it seems that most of the unhappy people we meet with are become so by neglect of that caution.

You ask what I mean? You love stories, and will excuse my telling one of myself.

When I was a child of seven years old, my friends, on a holiday, filled my pocket with coppers. I went directly to a shop where they sold toys for children; and, being charmed with the sound of a whistle that I met by the way in the hands of another boy, I voluntarily offered and gave all my money for one. I then came home and went whistling all over the house, much pleased with my whistle, but disturbing all the family. My brothers, and sisters, and cousins, understanding the bargain I had made, told me I had given four times as much for it as it was worth; put me in mind of what good things I might have bought with the rest of the money; and laughed at me so much for my folly, that I cried with vexation; and the reflection gave me more chagrin than the whistle gave me pleasure.

This, however, was afterward of use to me, the impression continuing on my mind; so that often, when I was tempted to buy some unnecessary thing, I said to myself, Don't give too much for the whistle; and I saved my money.

As I grew up, came into the world, and observed the actions of men, I thought I met with many, very many, who gave too much for the whistle.

When I saw one too ambitious of court favor, sacrificing his time in attendance on levees, his repose, his liberty, his virtue, and perhaps his friends, to attain it, I have said to myself, This man gives too much for his whistle.

When I saw another fond of popularity, constantly employing himself in political bustles, neglecting his own affairs, and ruining them by that neglect, He pays, indeed, said I, too much for his whistle.

If I knew a miser, who gave up every kind of comfortable living, all the pleasure of doing good to others, all the esteem of his fellow-citizens, and the joys of benevolent friendship, for the sake of accumulating wealth, Poor man, said I, you pay too much for your whistle.

When I met with a man of pleasure, sacrificing every laudable improvement of the mind or of his fortune to mere corporeal sensations, and ruining his health in their pursuit, Mistaken man, said I, you are providing pain for yourself instead of pleasure; you give too much for your whistle.

If I see one fond of appearance, or fine clothes, fine houses, fine furniture, fine equipages, all above his fortune, for which he contracts debts and ends his days in prison, Alas! say I, he has paid dear, very dear, for his whistle.

When I see a beautiful, sweet-tempered girl married to an ill-natured brute of a husband, What a pity, say I, that she should pay so much for a whistle!

In short, I conceive that great part of the miseries of mankind are brought upon them by the false estimates they have made of the value of things, and by their giving too much for their whistles.

Yet I ought to have charity for these unhappy people, when I consider that, with all this wisdom of which I am boasting, there are certain things in the world so tempting, for example, the apples of King John, which, happily, are not to be bought; for if they were put to sale by auction, I might very easily be led to ruin myself in the purchase, and find that I had once more given too much for the whistle.

Adieu, my dear friend, and believe me ever yours very sincerely and with unalterable affection,

B. Franklin

Light purse, heavy heart.

Necessity never made a good bargain.

NECESSARY HINTS TO THOSE THAT WOULD BE RICH

Written Anno 1736

The use of money is all the advantage there is in having money.

For six pounds a year you may have the use of one hundred pounds, provided you are a man of known prudence and honesty.

He that spends a groat a day idly, spends idly above six pounds a year, which is the price for the use of one hundred pounds.

He that wastes idly a groat's worth of his time per day, one day with another, wastes the privilege of using one hundred pounds each day.

He that idly loses five shillings' worth of time, loses five shillings, and might as prudently throw five shillings into the sea.

He that loses five shillings, not only loses that sum, but all the advantage that might be made by turning it in dealing, which, by the time that a young man becomes old, will amount to a considerable sum of money.

Again: he that sells upon credit, asks a price for what he sells equivalent to the principal and interest of his money for the time he is to be kept out of it; therefore, he that buys upon credit pays interest for what he buys, and he that pays ready money might let that money out to use: so that he that possesses anything he bought, pays interest for the use of it.

Yet, in buying goods, it is best to pay ready money, because he that sells upon credit expects to lose five percent by bad debts; therefore he charges, on all he sells upon credit, an advance that shall make up that deficiency.

Those who pay for what they buy upon credit, pay their share of this advance.

He that pays ready money escapes, or may escape, that charge.

A penny saved is twopence clear, A pin a day's a groat a year.

All things are cheap to the saving, dear to the wasteful.

The art of getting riches consists very much in thrift.

All men are not equally qualified for getting money, But it is in the power of every one alike to practice this virtue.

THE WAY TO MAKE MONEY PLENTY IN EVERY MAN'S POCKET

At this time, when the general complaint is that "money is scarce," it will be an act of kindness to inform the moneyless how they may reinforce their pockets. I will acquaint them with the true secret of money-catching, the certain way to fill empty purses, and how to keep them always full. Two simple rules, well observed, will do the business.

First, let honesty and industry be thy constant companions; and,

Secondly, spend one penny less than thy clear gains.

Then shall thy hidebound pocket soon begin to thrive, and will never again cry with the empty bellyache: neither will creditors insult thee, nor want oppress, nor hunger bite, nor nakedness freeze thee. The whole hemisphere will shine brighter, and pleasure spring up in every corner of thy heart. Now, therefore, embrace these rules and be happy. Banish the bleak winds of sorrow from thy mind, and live independent. Then shalt thou be a man, and not hide thy face at the approach of the rich, nor suffer the pain of feeling little when the sons of fortune walk at thy right hand: for independence, whether with little or much, is good fortune, and placeth thee on even ground with the proudest of the golden fleece. Oh, then, be wise, and let industry walk with thee in the morning, and attend thee until thou reachest the evening hour for rest. Let honesty be as the breath of thy soul, and never forget to have a penny when all thy expenses are enumerated and paid: then shalt thou reach the point of happiness, and independence shall be thy shield and buckler, thy helmet and crown; then shall thy soul walk upright, nor stoop to the silken wretch because he hath riches, nor

pocket an abuse because the hand which offers it wears a ring set with diamonds.

He that buys by the penny, maintains
not only himself, but other people.

Light Gains, heavy Purses.

ADVICE TO A YOUNG TRADESMAN

To My Friend, A. B.

As you have desired it of me, I write the following hints, which have been of service to me, and may, if observed, be so to you.

Remember that time is money. He that can earn ten shillings a day by his labor and goes abroad or sits idle one-half of that day, though he spends but sixpence during his diversion or idleness, ought not to reckon that the only expense; he has really spent, or rather thrown away, five shillings besides.

Remember that credit is money. If a man lets his money lie in my hands after it is due, he gives me the interest, or so much as I can make of it during that time. This amounts to a considerable sum where a man has good and large credit and makes good use of it.

Remember that money is of the prolific, generating nature. Money can beget money, and its offspring can beget more, and so on. Five shillings turned is six; turned again it is seven and threepence, and so on till it becomes a hundred pounds. The more there is of it the more it produces every turning, so that the profits rise quicker and quicker. He that kills a breeding sow destroys all her offspring to the thousandth generation. He that murders a crown destroys all that might have produced even scores of pounds.

Remember that six pounds a year is but a groat a day. For this little sum (which may be daily wasted either in time or expense unperceived) a man of credit may, on his own security, have the constant possession and use of a hundred pounds. So much in stock briskly turned by an industrious man produces great advantage.

Remember this saying, The good paymaster is lord of another man's purse. He that is known to pay punctually and exactly to the time he promises may at any time and on any occasion raise all the money his friends can spare.

This is sometimes of great use. After industry and frugality, nothing contributes more to the raising of a young man in the world than punctuality and justice in all his dealings; therefore never keep borrowed money an hour beyond the time you promised, lest a disappointment shut up your friend's purse forever.

The most trifling actions that affect a man's credit are to be regarded. The sound of your hammer at five in the morning or nine at night heard by a creditor makes him easy six months longer, but if he sees you at a billiard-table or hears your voice at a tavern, when you should be at work, he sends for his money the next day; demands it, before he can receive it, in a lump.

It shows, besides, that you are mindful of what you owe; it makes you appear a careful as well as an honest man, and that still increases your credit.

Beware of thinking all your own that you possess and of living accordingly. It is a mistake that many people who have credit fall into. To prevent this, keep an exact account for some time, both of your expenses and your income. If you take the pains at first to mention particulars, it will have this good effect: you will discover how wonderfully small, trifling expenses mount up to large sums, and will discern what might have been and may for the future be saved without occasioning any great inconvenience.

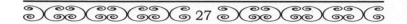

In short, the way to wealth, if you desire it, is as plain as the way to market. It depends chiefly on two words, industry and frugality; that is, waste neither time nor money, but make the best use of both. Without industry and frugality nothing will do, and with them everything. He that gets all he can honestly and saves all he gets (necessary expenses excepted) will certainly become rich, if that Being who governs the world, to whom all should look for a blessing on their honest endeavors, doth not, in his wise providence, otherwise determine.

An Old Tradesman

Early to bed and early to rise,
makes a man healthy, wealthy, and wise.

Pay what you owe, and
what you're worth you'll know.

ON LUXURY, IDLENESS, AND INDUSTRY[1]

It is wonderful how preposterously the affairs of this world are managed. Naturally one would imagine that the interest of a few individuals should give way to general interest; but individuals manage their affairs with so much more application, industry, and address than the public do theirs, that general interest most commonly gives way to particular. We assemble parliaments and councils to have the benefit of their collected wisdom; but we necessarily have, at the same time, the inconvenience of their collected passions, prejudices, and private interests. By the help of these, artful men overpower their wisdom and dupe its possessors: and if we may judge by the acts, arêtes, and edicts, all the world over, for regulating commerce, an assembly of great men is the greatest fool upon earth.

I have not yet, indeed, thought of a remedy for luxury. I am not sure that in a great state it is capable of a remedy, nor that the evil is in itself always so great as it is represented. Suppose we include in the definition of luxury all unnecessary expense, and then let us consider whether laws to prevent such expense are possible to be executed in a great country, and whether, if they could be executed, our people generally would be happier, or even richer. Is not the hope of being one day able to purchase and enjoy luxuries a great spur to labor and industry? May not luxury, therefore, produce more than it consumes, if without such a spur people would be, as they are naturally enough inclined to be, lazy and indolent! To this purpose I remember a circumstance. The skipper of a shallop, employed between Cape May and Philadelphia, had done us some small service, for which he refused to be paid. My wife, understanding that he had a daughter, sent her a new-fashioned cap. Three years after, this skipper being at my house with an old farmer of Cape May, his passenger, he mentioned the cap, and how much his daughter had been pleased with it. "But," said he, "it proved a dear cap to our congregation." "How so?" When my daughter appeared with it at meeting, it was so much admired that all the girls resolved to get such caps from Philadelphia; and my wife and I computed that the whole could not have cost less than a hundred pounds." "True," said the farmer, "but you do not tell all the story. I think the cap was, nevertheless, an advantage to us, for it was the first thing that put our girls upon knitting worsted mittens for sale at Philadelphia, that they might have wherewithal to buy caps and ribbons there; and you know that that industry has continued, and is likely to continue, and increase to a much greater value, and answer better purposes." Upon the whole, I was more reconciled to this little piece of luxury, since not only the girls were made happier by having fine caps, but the Philadelphians by the supply of warm mittens.

In our commercial towns upon the seacoast fortunes will occasionally be made. Some of those who grow rich will be prudent, live within bounds, and preserve what they have gained for their posterity; others, fond of showing their wealth, will be extravagant and ruin themselves. Laws cannot prevent this; and perhaps it is not always an evil to the public. A shilling spent idly by a fool may be picked up by a wiser person, who knows better what to do with it. It is, therefore, not lost. A vain, silly fellow builds a fine house, furnishes it richly, lives in it expensively, and in a few years ruins himself; but the masons, carpenters, smiths, and other honest tradesmen have been by his employ assisted in maintaining and raising their families; the farmer has been paid for his labor, and encouraged, and the estate is now in better hands. In some cases, indeed, certain modes of luxury may be a public evil, in the same manner as it is a private one. If there be a nation, for instance, that exports its beef and linen to pay for the importation of claret and porter, while a great part of its people live upon potatoes and wear no shirts, wherein does it differ from the sot, who lets his family starve and sells his clothes to buy drink? Our American commerce is, I confess, a little in this way. We sell our victuals to the Islands for rum and sugar; the substantial necessaries of life for superfluities. But we have plenty, and live well, nevertheless, though, by being soberer, we might be richer.

The vast quantity of forest-land we have yet to clear and put in order for cultivation, will for a long time keep the body of our nation laborious and frugal. Forming an opinion of our people and their manners, by what is seen among the inhabitants of the seaports, is judging from an improper sample. The people of the trading towns may be rich and luxurious, while the country possesses all the virtues that tend to promote happiness and public prosperity. Those towns are not much regarded by the country; they are hardly considered as an essential part of the states; and the experience of the last war has shown, that their being in possession of the enemy did not necessarily draw on the subjection of the country, which bravely continued to maintain its freedom and independence notwithstanding.

It has been computed by some political arithmetician, that if every man and woman would work for four hours every day on something useful, that labor would produce sufficient to procure all the necessaries of life, want and misery would be banished out of the world, and the rest of the twenty-four hours might be leisure and pleasure.

What occasions, then, so much want and misery? It is the employment of men and women in works that produce neither the necessaries nor conveniences of life; who, with those who do nothing, consume necessaries raised by the laborious to explain this.

The first elements of wealth are obtained by labor, from the earth and waters. I have land and raise corn. With this, if I feed a family that does nothing, my corn will be consumed, and at the end of the year I shall be no richer than I was at the beginning. But if, while I feed them, I employ them, some in spinning, others in making bricks, &c, for building, the value of my corn will be arrested and remain with me, and at the end of the year we may all be better clothed and better lodged. And if, instead of employing a man I feed in making bricks, I employ him in fiddling for me, the corn he eats is gone, and no part of his manufacture remains to augment the wealth and convenience of the family; I shall, therefore, be the poorer for this fiddling man, unless the rest of my family work more or eat less, to make up the deficiency he occasions.

Look round the world and see the millions employed in doing nothing, or in something that amounts to nothing, when the necessaries and conveniences of life are in question. What is the bulk of commerce, for which we fight and destroy each other, but the toil of millions for superfluities, to the great hazard and loss of many lives by the constant dangers of the sea? How much labor is spent in building and fitting great ships to go to China and Arabia for tea and coffee, to the West Indies for sugar, to America for tobacco? These things cannot be called the necessaries of life, for our ancestors lived very comfortably without them.

A question may be asked: Could all these people, now employed in raising, making, or carrying superfluities, be subsisted by raising necessaries? I think they might. The world is large, and a great part of it still uncultivated. Many hundred millions of acres in Asia, Africa, and America are still in a forest, and a great deal even in Europe. On a hundred acres of this forest a man might become a substantial farmer; and a hundred thousand men, employed in clearing each his hundred acres, would hardly brighten a spot big enough to be visible from the moon, unless with Herschel's telescope; so vast are the regions still in wood.

It is, however, some comfort to reflect, that, upon the whole, the quantity of industry and prudence among mankind exceeds the quantity of idleness and folly. Hence the increase of good buildings, farms cultivated, and populous cities filled with wealth, all over Europe, which a few ages since were only to be found on the coast of the Mediterranean; and this, notwithstanding the mad wars continually raging, by which are often destroyed in one year the works of many years' peace. So that we may hope the luxury of a few merchants on the coast will not be the ruin of America.

One reflection more, and I will end this long, rambling letter. Almost all the parts of our bodies require some expense. The feet demand shoes; the legs stockings; and the rest of the body clothing; and the belly a good deal of victuals. Our eyes, though exceedingly useful, ask, when reasonable, only the cheap assistance of spectacles, which could not much impair our finances. But the eyes of other people are the eyes that ruin us. If all but myself were

blind, I should want neither fine clothes, fine houses, nor fine furniture.

Ambition often spends foolishly
what Avarice had wickedly collected.

Diligence overcomes Difficulties,
Sloth makes them.

ON SMUGGLING, AND ITS VARIOUS SPECIES

Sir,

There are many people that would be thought, and even think themselves, honest men, who fail nevertheless in particular points of honesty; deviating from that character sometimes by the prevalence of mode or custom, and sometimes through mere inattention, so that their honesty is partial only, and not general or universal. Thus one who would scorn to overreach you in a bargain, shall make no scruple of tricking you a little now and then at cards: another, that plays with the utmost fairness, shall with great freedom cheat you in the sale of a horse. But there is no kind of dishonesty into which otherwise good people more easily and frequently fall, than that of defrauding government of its revenues by smuggling when they have an opportunity, or encouraging smugglers by buying their goods.

I fell into these reflections the other day, on hearing two gentlemen of reputation discoursing about a small estate, which one of them was inclined to sell and the other to buy; when the seller, in recommending the place, remarked, that its situation was very advantageous on this account, that, being on the seacoast in a smuggling country, one had frequent opportunities of buying many of the expensive articles used in a family (such as tea, coffee, chocolate, brandy, wines, cambrics, Brussels laces, French silks, and all kinds of India goods) 20, 30, and, in some articles, 50 percent cheaper than they could be had in the more interior parts, of traders that paid duty. The other honest gentleman allowed this to be an advantage, but insisted that the seller, in the advanced price he demanded on that account, rated the advantage much above its value. And neither of them seemed to think dealing with smugglers a practice that an honest man (provided he got his goods cheap) had the least reason to be ashamed of.

At a time when the load of our public debt, and the heavy expense of maintaining our fleets and armies to be ready for our defense on occasion, makes it necessary not only to continue old taxes, but often to look out for new ones, perhaps it may not be unuseful to state this matter in a light that few seem to have considered it in.

The people of Great Britain, under the happy constitution of this country, have a privilege few other countries enjoy, that of choosing the third branch of the legislature, which branch has alone the power of regulating their taxes. Now, whenever the government finds it necessary for the common benefit, advantage, and safety of the nation, for the security of our liberties, property, religion, and everything that is dear to us, that certain sums shall be yearly raised by taxes, duties, etc., and paid into the public treasury, thence to be dispensed by government for those purposes, ought not every honest man freely and willingly to pay his just proportion of this necessary expense? Can he possibly preserve a right to that character, if by fraud, stratagem, or contrivance, he avoids that payment in whole or in part?

What should we think of a companion who, having supped with his friends at a tavern, and partaken equally of the joys of the evening with the rest of us, would nevertheless contrive by some artifice to shift his share of the reckoning upon others, in order to go off scot-free? If a man who practiced this would, when detected, be deemed and called a scoundrel, what ought he to be called who can enjoy all the inestimable benefits of public society, and yet, by smuggling or dealing with smugglers, contrive to evade paying his just share of the expense, as settled by his own representatives in parliament, and wrongfully throw it upon his honest and, perhaps, much poorer neighbors? He will, perhaps, be ready to tell me that he does not wrong his neighbors; he scorns the imputation; he only cheats the king a little, who is very able to bear it. This, however, is a mistake. The public treasure is the treasure of the nation, to be applied to national purposes. And when a duty is laid for a particular public and necessary purpose, if, through smuggling, that duty falls short of raising the sum required, and other duties must therefore be laid to make up the deficiency, all the additional sum laid by the new duties and paid by other people, though it should amount to no more than a halfpenny or a farthing per lead, is so much actually picked out of the pockets of those other people by the smugglers and their abettors and encouragers. Are they, then, any better or other than pickpockets? And what mean, low, rascally pickpockets must those be that can pick pockets, for halfpence and for farthings?

I would not, however, be supposed to allow, in what I have just said, that cheating the king is a less offence against honesty than cheating the public. The king and the public, in this case, are different names for the same thing; but if we consider the king distinctly it will not lessen the crime: it is no justification of a robbery, that the person robbed was rich and able to bear it. The king has as much right to justice as the meanest of his subjects; and as he is truly the common father of his people, those that rob him fall under the scripture woe, pronounced against the son what robbeth his father and saith it is no sin.

Mean as this practice is, do we not daily see people of character and fortune engaged in it for trifling advantages to themselves? Is any lady ashamed to request of a gentleman of her acquaintance, that, when he returns from abroad, he would smuggle her home a piece of silk or lace from France or Flanders? Is any gentleman ashamed to undertake and execute the commission? Not in the least. They will talk of it freely, even before others -whose pockets they are thus contriving to pick by this piece of knavery.

Among other branches of the revenue, that of the post office is, by a late law, appropriated to the discharge of our public debt, to defray the expenses of the state. None but members of parliament and a few public officers have now a right to avoid, by a frank, the payment of postage. When any letter, not written by them or on their business, is franked by any of them, it is a hurt to the revenue, or injury which they must now take the pains to conceal by writing the whole superscription themselves. And yet such is our insensibility to justice in this particular, that nothing is more common than to see, even in a reputable company, a very honest gentleman or lady declare his or her intention to cheat the nation of threepence by a frank, and, without blushing, apply to one of the very legislators themselves, with a modest request that he would be pleased to become an accomplice in the crime and assist in the perpetration.

There are those who, by these practices, take a great deal in a year out of the public purse, and put the money into their own private pockets. If, passing through a room where public treasure is deposited, a man takes the opportunity of clandestinely pocketing and carrying off a guinea, is he not truly and properly a thief? And if another evades paying into the treasury a guinea he ought to pay in, and

applies it to his own use, when he knows it belongs to the public as much as that which has been paid in, what difference is there in the nature of the crime or the baseness of committing it?

Avoid dishonest gain: no price
can recompence the pangs of vice.

Speak little, do much.

ON TRUTH AND FALSEHOOD

Veritas luce clarior [2]

A friend of mine was the other day cheapening some trifles at a shopkeeper's, and after a few words they agreed on a price. At the tying up of the parcels he had purchased, the mistress of the shop told him that people were growing very hard, for she actually lost by everything she sold. How, then, is it possible, said my friend, that you can keep on your business? Indeed, sir, answered she, I must of necessity shut my doors, had I not a very great trade. The reason, said my friend (with a sneer), is admirable.

There are a great many retailers who falsely imagine that being historical (the modern phrase for lying) is much for their advantage; and some of them have a saying, that it is a pity lying is a sin, it is so useful in trade; though if they would examine into the reason why a number of shopkeepers raise considerable estates, while others who have set out with better fortunes have become bankrupts, they would find that the former made up with truth, diligence, and probity, what they were deficient of in stock; while the latter have been found guilty of imposing on such customers as they found had no skill in the quality of their goods.

The former character raises a credit which supplies the want of fortune, and their fair dealing brings them customers; whereas none will return to buy of him by whom he has been once imposed upon. If people in trade would judge rightly, we might buy blindfolded, and they would save, both to themselves and customers, the unpleasantness of haggling.

Though there are numbers of shopkeepers who scorn the mean vice of lying, and whose word may very safely be relied on, yet there are too many who will endeavor, and backing their falsities with asseverations, pawn their salvation to raise their prices.

As example works more than precept, and my sole view being the good and interest of my countrymen, whom I could wish to see without any vice or folly, I shall offer an example of the veneration bestowed on truth and abhorrence of falsehood among the ancients.

Augustus, triumphing over Mark Antony and Cleopatra, among other captives who accompanied them, brought to Rome a priest of about sixty years old; the senate being informed that this man had never been detected in a falsehood, and was believed never to have told a lie, not only restored him to liberty, but made him a high priest, and caused a statue to be erected to his honor. The priest thus honored was an Egyptian, and an enemy to Rome, but his virtue removed all obstacles.

Pamphilius was a Roman citizen, whose body upon his death was forbidden sepulture, his estate was confiscated, his house razed, and his wife and children banished to the Roman territories, wholly for his having been a notorious and inveterate liar.

Could there be greater demonstrations of respect for truth than these of the Romans, who elevated an enemy to the greatest honors, and exposed the family of a citizen to the greatest contumely?

There can be no excuse for lying, neither is there anything equally despicable and dangerous as a liar, no man being safe who associates with him; for he who will lie will swear to it, says the proverb; and such a one may endanger my life, turn my family out of doors, and ruin my reputation, whenever he shall find it his interest; and if a man will lie and swear to it in his shop to obtain a trifle, why should we doubt his doing so when he may hope to make a fortune by his perjury? The crime is in itself so mean, that to call a man a liar is esteemed everywhere an affront not to be forgiven.

If any have lenity enough to allow the dealers an excuse for this bad practice, I believe they will allow none for the gentleman who is addicted to this vice; and must look upon him with contempt. That the world does so, is visible by the derision with which his name is treated whenever it is mentioned.

The philosopher Epimenides gave the Rhodians this description of Truth: She is the companion of the gods, the joy of heaven, the light of the earth, the pedestal of justice, and the basis of good policy.

Eschines told the same people, that truth was a virtue without which force was enfeebled, justice corrupted;

humility became dissimulation, patience intolerable, chastity a dissembler, liberty lost, and pity superfluous.

Pharmanes the philosopher told the Romans that truth was the centre on which all things rested: a chart to sail by, a remedy for all evils, and a light to the whole world.

Anaxarchus, speaking of truth, said it was health incapable of sickness, life not subject to death, an elixir that healeth all, a sun not to be obscured, a moon without eclipse, an herb which never withereth, a gate that is never closed, and a path which never fatigues the traveler.

But if we are blind to the beauties of truth, it is astonishing that we should not open our eyes to the inconvenience of falsity. A man given to romance must be always on his guard, for fear of contradicting and exposing himself to derision; for the most historical would avoid the odious character, though it is impossible, with the utmost circumspection, to travel long on this route without detection, and shame and confusion follow. Whereas he who is a votary of truth never hesitates for an answer, has never to rack his invention to make the sequel quadrate with the beginning of his story, nor obliged to burden his memory with minute circumstances, since truth speaks easily what it recollects, and repeats openly and frequently without varying facts,

which liars cannot always do, even though gifted with a good memory.

Money & Man a mutual Friendship show:
Man makes false Money, Money makes Man so.

You will be careful, if you are wise,
How you touch men's Religion, or Credit, or Eyes.

ON THE USEFULNESS OF MATHEMATICS

Mathematics originally signifies any kind of discipline or learning, but now it is taken for that science which teaches or contemplates whatever is capable of being numbered or measured. That part of the mathematics which relates to numbers only, is called arithmetic; and that which is concerned about measure in general, whether length, breadth, motion, force, etc. is called geometry.

As to the usefulness of arithmetic, it is well-known that no business, commerce, trade, or employment whatsoever, even from the merchant to the shopkeeper, etc. can be managed and carried on without the assistance of numbers; for by these the trader computes the value of all sorts of goods that he dealeth in, does his business with ease and certainty, and informs himself how matters stand at any time with respect to men, money, or merchandise, to profit and loss, whether he goes forward or backward, grows richer or poorer. Neither is this science only useful to the merchant, but is reckoned the pritnum mobile (or first mover) of all mundane affairs in general, and is useful for all sorts and degrees of men, from the highest to the lowest.

As to the usefulness of geometry, it is as certain that no curious art, or mechanic work, can either be invented, improved, or performed, without its assisting principles.

It is owing to this, that astronomers are put into a way of making their observations, coming at the knowledge of the extent of the heavens, the duration of time, the motions, magnitudes, and distances of the heavenly bodies, their situations, positions, risings, settings, aspects, and eclipses; also the measure of seasons, of years, and of ages.

It is by the assistance of this science that geographers present to our view at once the magnitude and form of the whole earth, the vast extent of the seas, the divisions of empires, kingdoms, and provinces.

It is by the help of geometry the ingenious mariner is instructed how to guide a ship through the vast ocean, from one part of the earth to another, the nearest and safest way, and in the shortest time.

By help of this science the architects take their just measures for the structure of buildings, as private houses, churches, palaces, ships, fortifications, etc.

By its help engineers conduct all their works, take the situation and plan of towns, forts, and castles, measure their distances from one another, and carry their measure into places that are only accessible to the eye.

From hence also is deduced that admirable art of drawing sun-dials on any plane howsoever situate, and for any part of the world, to point out the exact time of the day, sun's declination, altitude, amplitude, azimuth, and other astronomical matters.

By geometry the surveyor is directed how to draw a map of any country, to divide his lands, and to lay down and plot any piece of ground, and thereby discover the area in acres, rods, and perches. The gauger is instructed how to find the capacities or solid contents of all kinds of vessels, in barrels, gallons, bushels, etc. And the measurer is furnished with rules for finding the areas and contents of superficies and solids, and casting up all manner of workmanship. All these, and many more useful arts, too many to be enumerated here, wholly depend upon the aforesaid sciences, viz. arithmetic and geometry.

This science is descended from the infancy of the world, the inventors of which were the first propagators of human kind, as Adam, Noah, Abraham, Moses, and divers others.

There has not been any science so much esteemed and honored as this of the mathematics, nor with so much industry and vigilance become the care of great men, and labored in by the potentates of the world, viz. emperors, kings, princes, etc.

Mathematical demonstrations are a logic of as much or more use, than that commonly learned at schools, serving to a just formation of the mind, enlarging its capacity, and strengthening it so as to render the same capable of exact reasoning, and discerning truth from falsehood in all occurrences, even subjects not mathematical. For which reason it is said, the Egyptians, Persians, and Lacedaemonians, seldom elected any new kings, but such as had some knowledge in the mathematics; imagining those who had not men of imperfect judgments, and unfit to rule and govern.

Though Plato's censure, that those who did not understand the 117th proposition of the 13th book of Euclid's Elements, ought not to be ranked amongst rational creatures, was unreasonable and unjust; yet to give a man the character of universal learning, who is destitute of a competent knowledge in the mathematics, is no less so.

The usefulness of some particular parts of the mathematics in the common affairs of human life, has rendered some knowledge of them very necessary to a great part of mankind, and very convenient to all the rest that are any way conversant beyond the limits of their own particular callings.

Those whom necessity has obliged to get their bread by manual industry, where some degree of art is required to go along with it, and who have had some insight into these studies, have very often found advantages from them sufficient to reward the pains they were at in acquiring them. And whatever may have been imputed to some other studies, under the notion of insignificancy and loss of time, yet these, I believe, never caused repentance in any, except it was for their remissness in the prosecution of them. . .

Philosophers do generally affirm that human knowledge to be most excellent, which is conversant amongst the most excellent things. What science then can there be more noble, more excellent, more useful for men, more admirably high and demonstrative, than this of the mathematics?

I shall conclude with what Plato says, in the seventh book of his Republic, with regard to the excellence and usefulness of geometry, being to this purpose:

"Dear Friend—You see then that mathematics are necessary, because by the exactness of the method, we get a habit of using our minds to the best advantage : and it is remarkable, that all men being capable by nature to reason and understand the sciences, the less acute, by studying this, though useless to them in every other respect, will gain this advantage, that their minds will be improved in reasoning aright; for no study employs it more, nor makes it susceptible of attention so much; and those who we find have a mind worth cultivating, ought to apply themselves to this study."

He who multiplies Riches multiplies Cares.

A penny saved is two pence clear. A pin a day is a groat a year. Save and have.

ON THE PRICE OF CORN, AND THE MANAGEMENT OF THE POOR[3]

To Messieurs the Public,

I am one of that class of people that feeds you all, and at present abused by you all; in short, I am a farmer.

By your newspapers we are told that God had sent a very short harvest to some other countries of Europe. I thought this might be in favor of Old England, and that now we should get a good price for our grain, which would bring millions among us, and make us flow in money: that, to be sure, is scarce enough.

But the wisdom of government forbade the exportation.

Well, says I, then we must be content with the market price at home.

No, say my lords the mob, you sha'n't have that. Bring your corn to market if you dare; we'll sell it for you for less money, or take it for nothing.

Being thus attacked by both ends of the constitution, the head and tail of government, what am I to do?

Must I keep my corn in the barn, to feed and increase the breed of rats? Be it so; they cannot be less thankful than those I have been used to feed.

Are we farmers the only people to be grudged the profits of our honest labor? And why? One of the late scribblers against us gives a bill of fare of the provisions at my daughter's wedding, and proclaims to all the world that we had the insolence to eat beef and pudding! Has he not read the precept in the good book, thou shall not muzzle the mouth of the ox that treadeth out the corn; or does he think us less worthy of good living than our oxen?

Oh, but the manufacturers! the manufacturers they are to be favored, and they must have bread at a cheap rate!

Hark ye, Mr. Oaf: The farmers live splendidly, you say. And, pray, would you have them hoard the money they get? Their fine clothes and furniture, do they make themselves or for one another, and so keep the money among them? Or do they employ these your darling manufacturers, and so scatter it again all over the nation?

The wool would produce me a better price if it were suffered to go to foreign markets; but that, Messieurs the Public, your laws will not permit. It must be kept all at home, that our dear manufacturers may have it the cheaper. And then, having yourselves thus lessened our encouragement for raising sheep, you curse us for the scarcity of mutton!

I have heard my grandfather say, that the farmers submitted to the prohibition on the exportation of wool, being made to expect and believe that, when the manufacturer bought his wool cheaper, they should also have their cloth cheaper. But the deuce a bit. It has been growing dearer and dearer from that day to this. How so? Why, truly, the cloth is exported: and that keeps up the price.

Now if it be a good principle that the exportation of a commodity is to be restrained, that so our people at home may have it the cheaper, stick to that principle, and go thorough stitch with it. Prohibit the exportation of your cloth, your leather and shoes, your ironware, and your manufactures of all sorts, to make them all cheaper at home. And cheap enough they will be, I will warrant you, till people leave off making them.

Some folks seem to think they ought never to be easy till England becomes another Lubberland, where it is fancied the streets are paved with penny-rolls, the houses tiled with pancakes, and chickens, ready roasted, cry, Come eat me.

I say, when you are sure you have got a good principle, stick to it and carry it through. I hear it is said, that though it was necessary and right for the ministry to advise a prohibition of the exportation of corn, yet it was contrary to law; and also, that though it was contrary to law for the mob to obstruct wagons, yet it was necessary and right. Just the same thing to a title. Now they tell me an act of indemnity ought to pass in favor of the ministry, to secure them from the consequences of having acted illegally. If so, pass another in favor of the mob. Others say, some of the mob ought to be hanged, by way of example. If so— but to say no more than I have said before, when you are sure that you have a good principle, go through with it.

You say poor laborers cannot afford to buy bread at a high price, unless they had higher wages. Possibly. But how shall we farmers be able to afford our laborers higher wages, if you will not allow us to get, when we might have it, a higher price for our corn?

By all that I can learn, we should at least have had a guinea a quarter more if the exportation had been allowed. And this money England would have got from foreigners.

But, it seems, we farmers must take so much less, that the poor may have it so much cheaper.

This operates, then, as a tax for the maintenance of the poor. A very good thing, you will say. But I ask, why a partial tax? Why laid on us farmers only? If it be a good thing, pray, Messieurs the public, take your share of it, by indemnifying us a little out of your public treasury. In doing a good thing there is both honor and pleasure; you are welcome to your share of both.

For my own part, I am not so well satisfied of the goodness of this thing. I am for doing good to the poor, but I differ in opinion about the means. I think the best way of doing good to the poor is not making them easy in poverty, but leading or driving them out of it. In my youth I travelled much, and I observed in different countries that the more public provisions were made for the poor, the less they provided for themselves, and, of course, became poorer. And, on the contrary, the less was done for them, the more they did for themselves, and became richer. There is no country in the world where so many provisions are established for them; so many hospitals to receive them when they are sick or lame, founded and maintained by voluntary charities; so many almshouses for the aged of both sexes, together with a solemn general law made by the rich to subject their estates to a heavy tax for the support of

the poor. Under all these obligations, are our poor modest, humble, and thankful? And do they use their best endeavors to maintain themselves, and lighten our shoulders of this burden? On the contrary, I affirm that there is no country in the world in which the poor are more idle, dissolute, drunken, and insolent. The day you passed that act you took away from before their eyes the greatest of all induce-ments to industry, frugality, and sobriety, by giving them a dependence on somewhat else than a careful accumulation during youth and health, for support in age or sickness. In short, you offered a premium for the encouragement of idleness, and you should not now wonder that it has had its effect in the increase of poverty. Repeal this law, and you will soon see a change in their manners; Saint Monday and Saint Tuesday will soon cease to he holydays. Six days shall thou labor, though one of the old commandments, long treated as out of date, will again be looked upon as a respectable precept; industry will increase, and with it plenty among the lower people; their circumstances will mend, and more will be done for their happiness by inur-ing them to provide for themselves, than could be done by dividing all your estates among them.

Excuse me, Messieurs the public, if upon this interest-ing subject I put you to the trouble of reading a little of my nonsense; I am sure I have lately read a great deal of yours,

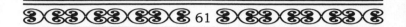

and therefore, from you (at least from those of you who are writers) I deserve a little indulgence. I am yours, &c,

Arator

Beware of little Expenses:
a small Leak will sink a great Ship.

He that waits upon fortune, is never sure of dinner.

AN ECONOMICAL PROJECT[4]

To the authors of the journal

Messieurs,

You often entertain us with accounts of new discoveries. Permit me to communicate to the public, through your paper, one that has lately been made by myself, and which I conceive may be of great utility.

I was the other evening in a grand company, where the new lamp of Messrs. Quinquet and Lange was introduced,

and much admired for its splendor; but a general enquiry was made, whether the oil it consumed, was not in proportion to the light it afforded, in which case there would be no saving in the use of it. No one present could satisfy us in that point, which all agreed ought to be known, it being a very desirable thing to lessen, if possible, the expense of lighting our apartments, when every other article of family expense was so much augmented.

I was pleased to see this general concern for economy; for I love economy exceedingly.

I went home, and to bed, three or four hours after midnight, with my head full of the subject. An accidental sudden noise waked me about six in the morning, when I was surprised to find my room filled with light; and I imagined at first that a number of those lamps had been brought into it: but rubbing my eyes, I perceived the light came in at the windows. I got up, and looked out to see what might be the occasion of it, when I saw the sun just rising above the horizon, from whence he poured his rays plentifully into my chamber, my domestic having negligently omitted the preceding evening to close the shutters.

I looked at my watch, which goes very well, and found that it was but six o'clock; and still thinking it something extraordinary that the sun should rise so early, I looked into the almanac; where I found it to be the hour given

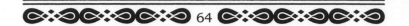

for his rising on that day. I looked forward too, and found he was to rise still earlier every day till towards the end of June; and that at no time in the year he retarded his rising so long as till eight o'clock. Your readers, who with me have never seen any signs of sunshine before noon, and seldom regard the astronomical part of the almanack, will be as much astonished as I was, when they hear of his rising so early; and especially when I assure them, that he gives light as soon as he rises. I am convinced of this. I am certain of the fact. One cannot be more certain of any fact. I saw it with my own eyes. And having repeated this observation the three following mornings, I found always precisely the same result.

Yet so it happens, that when I speak of this discovery to others, I can easily perceive by their countenances, though they forbear expressing it in words, that they do not quite believe me. One indeed, who is a learned natural philosopher, has assured me that I must certainly be mistaken as to the circumstance of the light coming into my room: for it being well known, as he says, that there could be no light abroad at that hour, it follows that none could enter from without; and that of consequence, my windows being accidentally left open, instead of letting in the light, had only served to let out the darkness: and he used many ingenious arguments to shew me how I

might, by that means, have been deceived. I own that he puzzled me a little, but he did not satisfy me; and the subsequent observations I made, as above mentioned, confirmed me in my first opinion.

This event has given rise, in my mind, to several serious and important reflections. I considered that if I had not been awakened so early in the morning, I should have slept six hours longer by the light of the sun, and in exchange have lived six hours the following night by candle light; and the latter being a much more expensive light than the former, my love of economy induced me to muster up what little arithmetic I was master of, and to make some calculations, which I shall give you, after observing, that utility is, in my opinion, the test of value in matters of invention, and that a discovery which can be applied to no use, or is not good for something, is good for nothing.

I took for the basis of my calculation the supposition that there are 100,000 families in Paris, and that these families consume in the night half a pound of bougies, or candles, per hour. I think this is a moderate allowance, taking one family with another; for though I believe some consume less, I know that many consume a great deal more. Then estimating seven hours per day, as the medium quantity between the time of the sun's rising and ours, he rising during the six following months from six to eight hours before noon,

and there being seven hours of course per night in which we burn candles, the account will stand thus—

In the six months between the
twentieth of March and the
twentieth of September, there
are nights   183
Hours of each night in which we
burn candles   7
Multiplication gives for the total
number of hours   1,281
These 1,281 hours multiplied by
100,000, the number of
inhabitants, give   128,100,000
One hundred twenty eight millions and
one hundred thousand hours,
spent at Paris by candle-light,
which, at half a pound of wax
and tallow per hour, gives the
weight of   64,050,000
Sixty-four millions and fifty thousand
of pounds, which, estimating
the whole at the medium price
of thirty sols the pound, makes
the sum of ninety-«ix millions

and seventy-five thousand
livres tournois   96,075,000

An immense sum! that the city of Paris might save every year, by the economy of using sunshine instead of candles.

If it should be said, that the people are apt to be obstinately attached to old customs, and that it will be difficult to induce them to rise before noon, consequently my discovery can be of little use; I answer, *Nil desperandum*. I believe all who have common sense, as soon as they have learnt from this paper that it is daylight when the sun rises, will contrive to rise with him; and, to compel the rest, I would propose the following regulations:

First: Let a tax be laid of a louis per window, on every window that is provided with shutters to keep out the light of the sun.

Second: Let the same salutary operation of police be made use of to prevent our burning candles, that inclined us last winter to be more economical in burning wood; that is, let guards be placed in the shops of the wax and tallow chandlers, and no family be permitted to be supplied with more than one pound of candles per week.

Third: Let guards be posted to stop all the coaches, etc., that would pass the streets after sunset, except those of physicians, surgeons, and midwives.

Fourth: Every morning, as soon as the sun rises, let all the bells in every church be set ringing; and if that is not sufficient, let cannon be fired in every street, and wake the sluggards effectually, and make them open their eyes to see their true interest.

All the difficulty will be in the first two or three days; after which the reformation will be as natural and as easy as the present irregularity: for *ce n' est que le premier pas qui coute*. Oblige a man to rise at four in the morning, and it is more than probable he shall go willingly to bed at eight in the evening ; and, having had eight hours sleep, he will rise more willingly at four the morning following. But this sum of ninety-six millions and seventy-five thousand livres is not the whole of what may be saved by my economical project. You may observe, that I have calculated upon only one half of the year, and much may be saved in the other, though the days are shorter. Besides, the immense stock of wax and tallow left unconsumed during the summer, will probably make candles much cheaper for the ensuing winter, and continue cheaper as long as the proposed reformation shall be supported.

For the great benefit of this discovery, thus freely communicated and bestowed by me on the public, I demand neither place, pension, exclusive privilege, nor any other reward whatever. I expect only to have the honor of it. And yet I know there are little envious minds who will, as usual, deny me this, and say that my invention was known to the ancients, and perhaps they may bring passages out of the old books in proof of it. I will not dispute with these people that the ancients knew not the sun would rise at certain hours; they possibly had, as we have, almanacs that predicted it: but it does not follow from thence that they knew he gave light as soon as he rose. This is what I claim as my discovery. If the ancients knew it, it must have long since been forgotten, for it certainly was unknown to the moderns, at least to the Parisians; which to prove, I need use but one plain simple argument. They are as well instructed, judicious, and prudent a people as exist anywhere in the world, all professing, like myself, to be lovers of economy; and, from the many heavy taxes required from them by the necessities of the state, have surely reason to be economical. I say it is impossible that so sensible a people, under such circumstances, should have lived so long by the smoky, unwholesome, and enormously expensive light of candles, if they had

really known; that they might have had as much pure light of the sun for nothing. I am, etc.

A Subscriber

If you'd be wealthy, think of saving, more than getting: The Indies have not made Spain rich, because her Outgoes equal her Incomes.

He that is rich need not live sparingly, and he that can live sparingly need not be rich.

The thrifty maxim of the wary Dutch, is to save all the money they can touch.

PLAN FOR SAVING ONE HUNDRED THOUSAND POUNDS

From *Poor Richard's Almanac*, 1756

As I spent some weeks last winter in visiting my old acquaintance in the Jerseys, great complaints I heard for want of money, and that leave to make more paper bills could not be obtained. Friends and Countrymen; my advice on this head shall cost you nothing ; and, if you will not be angry with me for giving it, I promise you not to be offended if you do not take it.

You spend yearly at least two hundred thousand pounds, it is said, in European, East-Indian, and West Indian commodities. Supposing one half of this expense to be in things absolutely necessary, the other half may be called superfluities, or, at best, conveniences, which, however, you might live without for one little year, and not suffer exceedingly. Now, to save this half, observe these few directions.

1. When you incline to have new clothes, look first well over the old ones, and see if you cannot shift with them another year, either by scouring, mending, or even patching if necessary. Remember, a patch on your coat, and money in your pocket, is better and more creditable, than a writ on your back, and no money to take it off.

2. When you incline to buy China ware, chintzes, India silks, or any other of their flimsy, slight manufactures, I would not be so hard with you, as to insist on your absolutely resolving against it; all I advise is, to put it off (as you do your repentance) till another year; and this, in some respects, may prevent an occasion of repentance.

3. If you are now a drinker of punch, wine, or tea, twice a day, for the ensuing year drink them but once a day. If you now drink them but once a day,

do it but every other day. If you do it now but once a week, reduce the practice to once a fortnight. And, if you do not exceed in quantity as you lessen the times, half your expense in these articles will be saved.

4. When you incline to drink rum, fill the glass half with water.

Thus at the year's end, there will be a hundred thousand pounds more money in your country.

If paper money in ever so great a quantity could be made, no man could get any of it without giving something for it. But all he saves in this way, will be his own for nothing, and his country actually so much richer. Then the merchants' old and doubtful debts may be honestly paid off, and trading become surer thereafter, if not so extensive.

Creditors have better memories than debtors.

Buy what thou hast no need of, and e'er
long thou shalt sell thy necessaries.

A MODEST ENQUIRY
INTO THE NATURE
AND NECESSITY OF
A PAPER CURRENCY[5]

Quid asper
Utile nummus habet; patriæ carisque propinquis
Quantum elargiri deceat.

Persius.

Philadelphia, April 3, 1729

There is no science, the study of which is more useful and commendable than the knowledge of the true interest of one's country; and perhaps there is no kind of learning more abstruse and intricate, more difficult to acquire in any degree of perfection than this, and therefore none more generally neglected. Hence it is, that we every day find men in conversation contending warmly on some point in politics, which, although it may nearly concern them both, neither of them understands any more than they do each other.

Thus much by way of apology for this present "Enquiry into the Nature and Necessity of a Paper Currency." And if anything I shall say may be a means of fixing a subject that is now the chief concern of my countrymen in a clearer light, I shall have the satisfaction of thinking my time and pains well employed.

To proceed, then,

There is a certain proportionate quantity of money requisite to carry on the trade of a country freely and currently; more than which would be of no advantage in trade, and less, if much less, exceedingly detrimental to it.

This leads us to the following general considerations.

First, a great want of money, in any trading country, occasions interest to be at a very high rate. And here it may be observed, that it is impossible by any laws to restrain men from giving and receiving exorbitant interest, where money is suitably scarce. For he that wants money will find out ways to give ten percent, when he cannot have it for less, although the law forbids to take more than six percent. Now the interest of money being high is prejudicial to a country several ways. It makes land bear a low price, because few men will lay out their money in land, when they can make a much greater profit by lending it out upon interest. And much less will men be inclined to venture their money at sea, when they can, without risk or hazard, have a great and certain profit by keeping it at home; thus trade is discouraged. And if in two neighboring countries the traders of one, by reason of a greater plenty of money, can borrow it to trade with at a lower rate than the traders of the other, they will infallibly have the advantage, and get the greatest part of that trade into their own hands; for he that trades with money he hath borrowed at eight or ten percent, cannot hold market with him that borrows his money at six or four. On the contrary, a plentiful currency will occasion interest to be low; and this will be an inducement to many to lay out their money in lands, rather than put it out to use, by which means land will begin to rise in value and bear a better price. And at the same time it will tend to enliven trade exceedingly, because people will find more profit in employing their money that way than in usury; and many that understand business very well, but have not a stock sufficient of their own, will be encouraged to borrow money to trade with, when they can have it at a moderate interest.

Secondly, want of money in a country reduces the price of that part of its produce which is used in trade; because, trade being discouraged by it as above, there is a much less demand for that produce. And this is another reason why land in such a case will be low, especially where the staple commodity of the country is the immediate produce of the land; because, that produce being low, fewer people find an advantage in husbandry, or the improvement of land. On the contrary, a plentiful currency will occasion the trading produce to bear a good price; because, trade being encouraged and advanced by it, there will be a much greater demand for that produce;[6] which will be a great encouragement of husbandry and tillage, and consequently make land more valuable, for that many people would apply themselves to husbandry, who probably might otherwise have sought some more profitable employment.

As we have already experienced how much the increase of our currency, by what paper money has been made, has encouraged our trade, particularly to instance only in one article, ship-building, it may not be amiss to observe under this head, what a great advantage it must be to us as a trading country, that has workmen and all the materials proper for that business within itself, to have ship-building as much as possible advanced; for every ship, that is built here for the English merchants, gains the province her clear value in gold and silver, which must otherwise have been sent home for returns in her stead; and likewise every ship, built in and belonging to the province, not only saves the province her first cost, but all the freight, wages, and provisions she ever makes or requires as long as she lasts; provided care is taken to make this her pay-port, and that she always takes provisions with her for the whole voyage, which may easily be done. And how considerable an article this is yearly in our favor, every one, the least acquainted with mercantile affairs, must needs be sensible; for, if we could not build ourselves, we must either purchase so many vessels as we want from other countries, or else hire them to carry our produce to market, which would be more expensive than purchasing, and on many other accounts exceedingly to our loss. Now as trade in general will decline where there is not a plentiful currency, so ship-building must certainly of consequence decline where trade is declining.

Thirdly, want of money in a country discourages laboring and handicraftsmen (who are the chief strength and support of a people) from coming to settle in it, and induces many that were settled to leave the country, and seek entertainment and employment in other places, where they can be better paid. For what can be more disheartening to an industrious laboring man than this, that, after he hath earned his bread with the sweat of his brows, he must spend as much time, and have near as much fatigue in getting it, as he had to earn it? And nothing makes more bad paymasters than a general scarcity of money. And here again is a third reason for land's bearing a low price in such a country, because land always increases in value in proportion with the increase of the people settling on it, there being so many more buyers; and its value will infallibly be diminished, if the number of its inhabitants diminish. On the contrary, a plentiful currency will encourage great numbers of laboring and handicraftsmen to come and settle in the country, by the same reason that a want of it will discourage and drive them out.[7] Now the more inhabitants, the greater demand for land (as is said above), upon which it must necessarily rise in value, and bear a better price. The same may be said of the value of house-rent, which will be advanced for the same reasons; and, by the increase of trade and riches, people will be enabled to pay greater rents. Now, the value of house-rent rising, and interest becoming low, many that in a scarcity of money practiced usury, will probably be more inclined to building; which will likewise sensibly enliven business in any place; it being an advantage not only to brick makers, bricklayers, masons, carpenters, joiners, glaziers, and several other trades immediately employed by building, but likewise to farmers, brewers, bakers, tailors, shoemakers, shopkeepers, and, in short, to every one that they lay their money out with.

Fourthly, want of money in such a country as ours, occasions a greater consumption of English and European goods, in proportion to the number of the people, than there would otherwise be. Because merchants and traders, by whom abundance of artificers and laboring men are employed, finding their other affairs require what money they can get into their hands, oblige those who work for them to take one half or perhaps two-thirds goods in pay. By this means a greater quantity of goods are disposed of, and to a greater value; because working-men and their families are thereby induced to be more profuse and extravagant in fine apparel and the like, than they would be if they were obliged to pay ready money for such things after they had earned and received it, or if such goods were not imposed upon them, of which they can make no other use. For such people cannot send the goods they are paid with to a foreign market, without losing considerably by having them sold for less than they stand them in here; neither can they easily dispose of them at home, because their neighbors are generally supplied in the same manner. But how unreasonable would it be, if some of those very men who have been a means of thus forcing people into unnecessary expense, should be the first and most earnest in accusing them of pride and prodigality. Now, though this extraordinary consumption of foreign commodities may be a profit to particular men, yet the country in general grows poorer by it apace. On the contrary, as a plentiful currency will occasion a less consumption of European goods, in proportion to the number of the people, so it will be a means of making the balance of our trade more equal than it now is, if it does not give it in our favor; because our own produce will be encouraged at the same time. And it is to be observed, that, though less foreign commodities are consumed in proportion to the number of people, yet this will be no disadvantage to the merchant, because the number of people increasing, will occasion an increasing demand of more foreign goods in the whole.

Thus we have seen some of the many heavy disadvantages a country (especially such a country as ours) must labor under, when it has not a sufficient stock of running cash to manage its trade currently. And we have likewise seen some of the advantages which accrue from having money sufficient, or a plentiful currency.

The foregoing paragraphs being well considered, we shall naturally be led to draw the following conclusions with regard to what persons will probably be for or against emitting a large additional sum of paper bills in this province.

1. Since men will always be powerfully influenced in their opinions and actions by what appears to be their particular interest, therefore all those, who, wanting courage to venture in trade, now practice lending money on security for exorbitant interest, which, in a scarcity of money will be done, notwithstanding the law, I say all such will probably be against a large addition to our present stock of paper money; because a plentiful currency will lower interest, and make it common to lend on less security.

2. All those who are possessors of large sums of money, and are disposed to purchase land, which is attended with a great and sure advantage in a growing country as this is; I say, the interest of all such men will incline them to oppose a large addition to our money. Because their wealth is now continually increasing by the large interest they receive, which will enable them (if they can keep land from

rising) to purchase more some time hence than they can at present; and in the meantime all trade being discouraged, not only those who borrow of them, but the common people in general will be impoverished, and consequently obliged to sell more land for less money than they will do at present. And yet, after such men are possessed of as much land as they can purchase, it will then be their interest to have money made plentiful, because that will immediately make land rise in value in their hands. Now it ought not to be wondered at, if people from the knowledge of a man's interest do sometimes make a true guess at his designs; for interest, they say, will not lie.

3. Lawyers, and others concerned in court business, will probably many of them be against a plentiful currency; because people in that case will have less occasion to run in debt, and consequently less occasion to go to law and sue one another for their debts. Though I know some even among these gentlemen, that regard the public good before their own apparent private interest.

4. All those who are any way dependents on such persons as are above mentioned, whether as holding offices, as tenants, or as debtors, must at least appear to be against a large addition; because, if they do not,

they must sensibly feel their present interest hurt. And besides these, there are, doubtless, many well-meaning gentlemen and others, who, without any immediate private interest of their own in view, are against making such an addition, through an opinion they may have of the honesty and sound judgment of some of their friends that oppose it (perhaps for the ends aforesaid), without having given it any thorough consideration themselves. And thus it is no wonder if there is a powerful party on that side.

On the other hand, those who are lovers of trade, and delight to see manufactures encouraged, will be for having a large addition to our currency. For they very well know, that people will have little heart to advance money in trade, when what they can get is scarce sufficient to purchase necessaries, and supply their families with provisions. Much less will they lay it out in advancing new manufactures; nor is it possible new manufactures should turn to any account, where there is not money to pay the workmen, who are discouraged by being paid in goods, because it is a great disadvantage to them.

Again, those who are truly for the proprietor's interest (and have no separate views of their own that are predominant), will be heartily for a large addition. Because, as I have shown above, plenty of money will for several reasons make land rise in value exceedingly. And I appeal to those immediately concerned for the proprietor in the sale of his lands, whether land has not risen very much since the first emission of what paper currency we now have, and even by its means. Now we all know the proprietary has great quantities to sell.

And since a plentiful currency will be so great a cause of advancing this province in trade and riches, and increasing the number of its people; which, though it will not sensibly lessen the inhabitants of Great Britain, will occasion a much greater vent and demand for their commodities here; and allowing that the crown is the more powerful for its subjects increasing in wealth and number, I cannot think it the interest of England to oppose us in making as great a sum of paper money here, as we, who are the best judges of our own necessities, find convenient. And if I were not sensible that the gentlemen of trade in England, to whom we have already parted with our silver and gold, are misinformed of our circumstances, and therefore endeavor to have our currency stinted to what it now is, I should think the government at home had some reasons for discouraging and impoverishing this province, which we are not acquainted with.

It remains now that we enquire, whether a large addition to our paper currency will not make it sink in value very much. And here it will be requisite that we first form just notions of the nature and value of money in general.

As Providence has so ordered it, that not only different countries, but even different parts of the same country, have their peculiar most suitable productions; and likewise that different men have geniuses adapted to a variety of different arts and manufactures; therefore commerce, or the exchange of one commodity or manufacture for another, is highly convenient and beneficial to mankind. As for instance, A may be skilful in the art of making cloth, and B understand the raising of corn. A wants corn, and B cloth; upon which they make an exchange with eachother for as much as each has occasion for, to the mutual advantage and satisfaction of both.

But as it would be very tedious, if there were no other way of general dealing, but by an immediate exchange of commodities; because a man that had corn to dispose of, and wanted cloth for it, might perhaps, in his search for a chapman to deal with, meet with twenty people that had cloth to dispose of, but wanted no corn; and with twenty others that wanted his corn, but had no cloth to suit him with; to remedy such inconveniences, and facilitate exchange, men have invented money, properly called a medium of exchange, because through or by its means labor is exchanged for labor, or one commodity for another. And whatever particular thing men have agreed to make this medium of, whether gold, silver, copper, or tobacco, it is, to those who possess it (if they want anything), that very thing which they want, because it will immediately procure it for them. It is cloth to him that wants cloth, and corn to those that want corn; and so of all other necessaries, it is whatsoever it will procure. Thus he who had corn to dispose of, and wanted to purchase cloth with it, might sell his corn, for its value in this general medium, to one who wanted corn but had no cloth; and with this medium he might purchase cloth of him that wanted no corn, but perhaps some other thing, as iron it may be, which this medium will immediately procure, and so he may be said to have exchanged his cloth for iron; and thus the general change is soon performed, to the satisfaction of all parties, with abundance of facility.

For many ages, those parts of the world which are engaged in commerce, have fixed upon gold and silver as the chief and most proper materials for this medium; they being in themselves valuable metals for their fineness, beauty, and scarcity. By these, particularly by silver, it has been usual to value all things else. But as silver itself is of no certain permanent value, being worth more or less according to its scarcity or plenty, therefore it seems requisite to fix upon something else, more proper to be made a measure of values, and this I take to be labor.[8]

By labor may the value of silver be measured as well as other things. As, suppose one man employed to raise corn, while another is digging and refining silver; at the year's end, or at any other period of time, the complete produce of corn, and that of silver, are the natural price of each other; and if one be twenty bushels, and the other twenty ounces, then an ounce of that silver is worth the labor of raising a bushel of that corn. Now if by the discovery of some nearer, more easy or plentiful mines, a man may get forty ounces of silver as easily as formerly he did twenty, and the same labor is still required to raise twenty bushels of corn, then two ounces of silver will be worth no more than the same labor of raising one bushel of corn, and that bushel of corn will be as cheap at two ounces, as it was before at one, cæteris paribus.

Thus the riches of a country are to be valued by the quantity of labor its inhabitants are able to purchase, and not by the quantity of silver and gold they possess; which will purchase more or less labor, and therefore is more or less valuable, as is said before, according to its scarcity or plenty. As those metals have grown much more plentiful in Europe since the discovery of America,[9] so they have sunk in value exceedingly; for, to instance in England, formerly one penny of silver was worth a day's labor, but now it is hardly worth the sixth part of a day's labor; because not less than sixpence will purchase the labor of a man for a day in any part of that kingdom; which is wholly to be attributed to the much greater plenty of money now in England than formerly. And yet perhaps England is in effect no richer now than at that time; because as much labor might be purchased, or work got done of almost any kind, for one hundred pounds then, as will now require or is now worth six hundred pounds.

In the next place let us consider the nature of banks emitting bills of credit, as they are at this time used in Hamburg, Amsterdam, London, and Venice.

Those places being seats of vast trade, and the payment of great sums being for that reason frequent, bills of credit are found very convenient in business; because a great sum is more easily counted in them, lighter in carriage, concealed in less room, and therefore safer in travelling or laying up, and on many other accounts they are very much valued. The banks are the general cashiers of all gentlemen, merchants, and great traders in and about those cities; there they deposit their money, and may take out bills to the value, for which they can be certain to have money again at the bank at any time. This gives the bills a credit; so that in England they are never less valuable than money, and in Venice and Amsterdam they are generally worth more. And the bankers, always reserving money in hand to answer more than the common run of demands (and some people constantly putting in while others are taking out), are able besides to lend large sums, on good security, to the government or others, for a reasonable interest, by which they are paid for their care and trouble; and the money, which otherwise would have lain dead in their hands, is made to circulate again thereby among the people. And thus the running cash of the nation is, as it were, doubled; for all great payments being made in bills, money in lower trade becomes much more plentiful. And this is an exceeding great advantage to a trading country, that is not overstocked with gold and silver.[10]

As those, who take bills out of the banks in Europe, put in money for security; so here, and in some of the neighboring provinces, we engage our land. Which of these methods will most effectually secure the bills from actually sinking in value, comes next to be considered.

Trade in general being nothing else but the exchange of labor for labor, the value of all things is, as I have said before, most justly measured by labor. Now suppose I put my money into a bank, and take out a bill for the value; if this bill at the time of my receiving it, would purchase me the labor of one hundred men for twenty days, but some time after will only purchase the labor of the same number of men for fifteen days, it is plain the bill has sunk in value one fourth part. Now, silver and gold being of no permanent value, and as this bill is founded on money, and therefore to be esteemed as such, it may be that the occasion of this fall is the increasing plenty of gold and silver, by which money is one fourth part less valuable than before, and therefore one fourth more is given of it for the same quantity of labor; and, if land is not become more plentiful by some proportionate decrease of the people, one fourth part more of money is given for the same quantity of land; whereby it appears, that it would have been more profitable to me to have laid that money out in land which I put into the bank, than to place it there and take a bill for it. And it is certain that the value of money has been continually sinking in England for several ages past, because it has been continually increasing in quantity. But, if bills could be taken out of a bank in Europe on a land security, it is probable the value of such bills would be more certain and steady, because the number of inhabitants continues to be near the same in those countries from age to age.

For, as bills issued upon money security are money, so bills issued upon land, are in effect coined land.

Therefore, (to apply the above to our own circumstances) if land in this province was falling, or any way likely to fall, it would behove the legislature most carefully to contrive how to prevent the bills issued upon land from falling with it. But, as our people increase exceedingly, and will be further increased, as I have before shown, by the help of a large addition to our currency, and as land in consequence is continually rising, so, in case no bills are emitted but what are upon land security, the money-acts in every part punctually enforced and executed, the payments of principal and interest being duly and strictly required, and the principal bond fide sunk according to law, it is absolutely impossible such bills should ever sink below their first value, or below the value of the land on which they are founded. In short, there is so little danger of their sinking, that they would certainly rise as the land rises, if they were not emitted in a proper manner for preventing it. That is, by providing in the act, that payment may be made, either in those bills, or in any other bills made current by any act of the legislature of this province; and that the interest, as it is received, may be again emitted in discharge of public debts; whereby circulating, it returns again into the hands of the borrowers, and becomes part of their future payments; and thus, as it is likely there will not be any difficulty for want of bills to pay the office, they are hereby kept from rising above their first value. For else, supposing there should be emitted upon mortgaged land its full present value in bills, as in the banks in Europe the full value of the money deposited is given out in bills; and supposing the office would take nothing but the same sum in those bills in discharge of the land, as, in the banks aforesaid, the same sum in their bills must be brought in, in order to receive out the money; in such case the bills would most surely rise in value as the land rises; as certainly as the bank bills founded on money would fall, if that money was falling. Thus, if I were to mortgage to a loan-office, or bank, a parcel of land now valued at one hundred pounds in silver, and receive for it the like sum in bills, to be paid in again at the expiration of a certain term of years, before which my land, rising in value, becomes worth one hundred and fifty pounds in silver; it is plain, that if I have not these bills in possession, and the office will take nothing but these bills, or else what it is now become worth in silver, in discharge of my land; I say it appears plain, that those bills will now be worth one hundred and fifty pounds in silver to the possessor; and if I can purchase them for less, in order to redeem my land, I shall by so much be a gainer.

I need not say anything to convince the judicious that our bills have not yet sunk, though there is and has been some difference between them and silver; because it is evident, that that difference is occasioned by the scarcity of the latter, which is now become a merchandise, rising and falling, like other commodities, as there is a greater or less demand for it, or as it is more or less plenty.

Yet farther, in order to make a true estimate of the value of money, we must distinguish between money as it is bullion, which is merchandise, and as by being coined it is made a currency. For its value as a merchandise, and its value as a currency, are two distinct things; and each may possibly rise and fall in some degree independent of the other. Thus, if the quantity of bullion increases in a country, it will proportionably decrease in value; but if at the same time the quantity of current coin should decrease, (supposing payments may not be made in bullion) what coin there is will rise in value as a currency; that is, people will give more labor in manufactures for a certain sum of ready money.

In the same manner must we consider a paper currency founded on land; as it is land, and as it is a currency.

Money as bullion, or as land, is valuable by so much labor as it costs to procure that bullion or land.

Money, as a currency, has an additional value by so much time and labor as it saves in the exchange of commodities.

If, as a currency, it saves one fourth part of the time and labor of a country it has, on that account, one fourth added to its original value.

When there is no money in a country, all commerce must be by exchange.[11] Now, if it takes one fourth part of the time and labor of a country, to exchange or get their commodities exchanged; then, in computing their value, that labor of exchanging must be added to the labor of manufacturing those commodities. But if that time or labor is saved by introducing money sufficient, then the additional value on account of the labor of exchanging may be abated, and things sold for only the value of the labor in making them; because the people may now in the same time make one fourth more in quantity of manufactures than they could before.

From these considerations it may be gathered, that in all the degrees between having no money in a country, and money sufficient for the trade, it will rise and fall in value as a currency, in proportion to the decrease or increase of its quantity. And if there may be at some time more than enough, the overplus will have no effect towards making the currency, as a currency, of less value than when there was but enough; because such overplus will not be used in trade, but be some other way disposed of.

If we enquire, how much percent interest ought to be required upon the loan of these bills, we must consider what is the natural standard of usury. And this appears to be, where the security is undoubted, at least the rent of so much land as the money lent will buy. For it cannot be expected, that any man will lend his money for less than it would fetch him in as rent if he laid it out in land, which is the most secure property in the world. But if the security is casual, then a kind of insurance must be interwoven with the simple natural interest, which may advance the usury very conscionably to any height below the principal itself. Now, among us, if the value of land is twenty years' purchase, five percent is the just rate of interest for money lent on undoubted security. Yet, if money grows scarce in a country, it becomes more difficult for people to make punctual payments of what they borrow, money being hard to be raised; likewise, trade being discouraged and business impeded for want of a currency, abundance of people must be in declining circumstances, and by these means security is more precarious than where money is plenty. On such accounts it is no wonder if people ask a greater interest for their money than the natural interest; and what is above is to be looked upon as a kind of premium for the insurance of those uncertainties, as they are greater or less. Thus we always see, that where money is scarce, interest is high, and low where it is plenty.[12] Now it is certainly the advantage of a country to make interest as low as possible, as I have already shown; and this can be done no other way than by making money plentiful. And since, in emitting paper money among us, the office has the best of security, the titles to the land being all skillfully and strictly examined and ascertained;

and as it is only permitting the people by law to coin their own land, which costs the government nothing, the interest being more than enough to pay the charges of printing, officers' fees, etc. I cannot see any good reason why four percent to the loan-office should not be thought fully sufficient. As a low interest may incline more to take money out, it will become more plentiful in trade; and this may bring down the common usury, in which security is more dubious, to the pitch it is determined at by law.

If it should be objected, that emitting it at so low an interest, and on such easy terms, will occasion more to be taken out than the trade of the country really requires; it may be answered, that, as has already been shown, there can never be so much of it emitted as to make it fall below the land it is founded on; because no man in his senses will mortgage his estate for what is of no more value to him than that he has mortgaged, especially if the possession of what he receives is more precarious than of what he mortgages, as that of paper money is when compared to land.[13]

And if it should ever become so plenty by indiscreet persons continuing to take out a large overplus, above what is necessary in trade, so as to make people imagine it would become by that means of less value than their mortgaged lands, they would immediately of course begin to pay it in again to the office to redeem their land, and continue to do so till there was no more left in trade than was absolutely necessary.[14] And thus the proportion would find itself (though there were a million too much in the office to be let out), without giving anyone the trouble of calculation.

It may, perhaps, be objected to what I have written concerning the advantages of a large addition to our currency, that, if the people of this province increase, and husbandry is more followed, we shall overstock the markets with our produce of flour, etc.[15] To this it may be answered, that we can never have too many people (nor too much money). For, when one branch of trade or business is overstocked with hands, there are the more to spare to be employed in another. So, if raising wheat proves dull, more may (if there is money to support and carry on new manufactures) proceed to the raising and manufacturing of hemp, silk, iron, and many other things the country is very capable of, for which we only want people to work, and money to pay them with.

Upon the whole it may be observed, that it is the highest interest of a trading country in general to make money plentiful; and that it can be a disadvantage to none that have honest designs. It cannot hurt even the usurers, though it should sink what they receive as interest; because they will be proportionably more secure in what they lend; or they will have an opportunity of employing their money to greater advantage, to themselves as well as to the country. Neither can it hurt those merchants, who have great sums outstanding in debts in the country, and seem on that account to have the most plausible reason to fear it; to wit, because a large addition being made to our currency will increase the demand of our exporting produce, and by that means raise the price of it, so that they will not be able to purchase so much bread or flour with one hundred pounds when they shall receive it after such an addition, as they now can, and may if there is no addition. I say it cannot hurt even such, because they will get in their debts just in exact proportion so much the easier and sooner as the money becomes plentier; and therefore, considering the interest and trouble saved, they will not be losers; because it only sinks in value as a currency, proportionally as it becomes more plenty. It cannot hurt the interest of Great Britain, as has been shown; and it will greatly advance the interest of the proprietor. It will be an advantage to every industrious tradesman, & etc., because his business will be carried on more freely, and trade be universally enlivened by it. And as more business in all manufactures will be done, by so much as the labor and time spent in exchange is saved, the country in general will grow so much the richer.

It is nothing to the purpose to object the wretched fall of the bills in New England and South Carolina, unless it might be made evident that their currency was emitted with the same prudence, and on such good security, as ours is; and it certainly was not.

As this essay is wrote and published in haste, and the subject in itself intricate, I hope I shall be censured with candor, if, for want of time carefully to revise what I have written, in some places I should appear to have expressed myself too obscurely, and in others am liable to objections I did not foresee. I sincerely desire to be acquainted with the truth, and on that account shall think myself obliged to anyone, who will take the pains to show me, or the public, where I am mistaken in my conclusions. And as we all know there are among us several gentlemen of acute parts and profound learning, who are very much against any addition to our money, it were to be wished that they would favor the country with their sentiments on this head in print; which, supported with truth and good reasoning, may probably be very convincing. And this is to be desired the rather because many people, knowing the abilities of those gentlemen to manage a good cause, are apt to construe their silence in this, as an argument of a bad one. Had anything of that kind ever yet appeared, perhaps I should not have given the public this trouble. But, as those ingenious gentlemen have not yet (and I doubt ever will) think it worth their concern to enlighten the minds of their

erring countrymen in this particular, I think it would be highly commendable in every one of us, more fully to bend our minds to the study of what is the true interest of Pennsylvania; whereby we may be enabled, not only to reason pertinently with one another; but, if occasion requires, to transmit home such clear representations, as must inevitably convince our superiors of the reasonableness and integrity of our designs.[16]

Haste makes Waste.

If you know how to spend less than you get, you have the philosopher's stone.

LETTERS TO
MRS. JANE MECOM

Woodbridge, East New Jersey, May 21, 1757

Dear Sister,

I received your kind letter of the 9th instant, in which you acquainted me with some of your late troubles. These are troublesome times to us all; but perhaps you have heard more than you should. I am glad to hear that Peter is at a place where he has full employ. A trade is a valuable thing; but unless a habit of industry be acquired with it, it turns out of little use; if he gets that in his new place, it will be a happy exchange, and the occasion not an unfortunate one.

It is very agreeable to me to hear so good an account of your other children; in such a number, to have no bad ones is a great happiness.

The horse sold very low indeed. If I wanted one tomorrow, knowing his goodness, old as he is, I should freely give more than twice the money for him; but you did the best you could, and I will take of Benny no more than he produced.

I don't doubt but Benny will do very well when he gets to work: but I fear his things from England may be so long a-coming as to occasion the loss of the rent. Would it not be better for you to move into the house? Perhaps not, if he is near being married. I know nothing of that affair but what you write me, except that I think Miss Betsey a very agreeable, sweet-tempered, good girl, who has had a housewifery education, and will make, to a good husband, a very good wife. Your sister and I have a great esteem for her, and if she will be kind enough to accept of our nephew, we think it will be his own fault if he is not as happy as the married state can make him.

The family is a respectable one, but whether there be any fortune I know not; and as you do not enquire about this particular, I suppose you think with me, that where everything else desirable is to be met with, that is not very material. If she does not bring a fortune she will have to make one. Industry, frugality, and prudent economy in a wife, are to a tradesman, in their effects, a fortune; and a fortune sufficient for Benjamin, if his expectations are reasonable. We can only add, that if the young lady and her friends are willing, we give our consent heartily and our blessing. My love to brother and the children concludes with me.

B. Franklin

New York, May 30, 1757

Dear Sister,

I have before me yours of the 9th and 16th instant. I am glad you have resolved to visit sister Dowse oftener; it will be a great comfort to her to find she is not neglected by you, and your example may, perhaps, be followed by some other of her relations.

As Neddy is yet a young man, I hope he may get over the disorder he complains of, and in time wear it out. My love to him and his wife and the rest of your children. It gives me pleasure to hear that Eben is likely to get into business at his trade. If he will be industrious and frugal, 'tis ten to one but he gets rich, for he seems to have spirit and activity.

I am glad that Peter is acquainted with the crown soap business, so as to make what is good of the kind. I hope he will always take care to make it faithfully, never slight manufacture, or attempt to deceive by appearances. Then he may boldly put his name and mark, and in a little time it will acquire as good a character as that made by his late uncle, or any other person whatever. I believe his aunt at Philadelphia can help him to sell a good deal of it; and I doubt not of her doing everything in her power to promote his interest in that way. Let a box be sent to her (but not unless it be right good), and she will immediately return the ready money for it. It was beginning once to be in vogue in Philadelphia, but brother John sent me one box, an ordinary sort, which checked its progress. I would not have him put the Franklin arms on it; but the soapboiler's arms he has a right to use, if he thinks fit. The other would look too much like an attempt to counterfeit. In his advertisements he may value himself on serving his time with the original maker, but put his own mark or device on the papers, or anything he may be advised as proper; only on the soap, as it is called by the name of crown soap, it seems necessary to use a stamp of that sort, and perhaps no soapboiler in the king's dominions has a better right to the crown than himself.

Nobody has wrote a syllable to me concerning his making use of the hammer, or made the least complaint of him or you. I am sorry, however, he took it without leave. It was irregular, and if you had not approved of his doing it I should have thought it indiscreet. Leave, they say, is light, and it seems to me a piece of respect that was due to his aunt to ask it, and I can scarce think she would have refused him the favour.

I am glad to hear Jamey is so good and diligent a workman; if he ever sets up at the goldsmith's business, he must remember that there is one accomplishment without which he cannot possibly thrive in that trade (i.e., to be perfectly honest). It is a business that, though ever so uprightly managed, is always liable to suspicion; and if a man is once detected in the smallest fraud it soon becomes public, and everyone is put upon their guard against him; no one will venture to try his hands, or trust him to make up their plate; so at once he is ruined. I hope my nephew will therefore establish a character as an honest and faithful as well as skilful workman, and then he need not fear employment.

And now, as to what you propose for Benny, I believe he may be, as you say, well enough qualified for it; and when he appears to be settled, if a vacancy should happen, it is very probable he may be thought of to supply it; but it is a rule with me not to remove any officer that behaves well, keeps regular accounts, and pays duly; and I think the rule is founded on reason and justice. I have not shown any backwardness to assist Benny, where it could be done without injuring another. But if my friends require of me to gratify not only their inclinations, but their resentments, they expect too much of me. Above all things, I dislike family quarrels; and when they happen among my relations, nothing gives me more pain. If I were to set myself up as a judge of those subsisting between you and brother's widow and children, how unqualified must I be, at this distance, to determine rightly, especially having heard but one side. They always treated me with friendly and affectionate regard; you have done the same. What can I say between you but that I wish you were reconciled, and that I will love that side best that is most ready to forgive and oblige the other. You will be angry with me here for putting

you and them too much upon a footing, but I shall
nevertheless be,

B. Franklin

The use of money is all the advantage
there is in having money.

LETTER TO
MISS STEVENSON,
WANSTEAD

Craven-street, May 16, 1760

I send my good girl the books I mentioned to her last night. I beg her to accept of them as a small mark of my esteem and friendship. They are written in the familiar, easy manner for which the French are so remarkable; and afford a good deal of philosophic and practical knowledge, nembarrassed with the dry mathematics used by more exact reasoners, but which is apt to discourage young beginners.

I would advise you to read with a pen in your hand, and enter in a little book short hints of what you find that is curious or that may be useful; for this will be the best method of imprinting such particulars in your memory, where they will be ready either for practice on some future occasion if they are matters of utility, or at least to adorn and improve your conversation if they are rather points of curiosity. And as many of the terms of science are such as you cannot have met with in your common reading, and may, therefore, be unacquainted with, I think it would be well for you to have a good dictionary at hand, to consult immediately when you meet with a word you do not comprehend the precise meaning of. This may at first seem troublesome and interrupting; but it is a trouble that will daily diminish, as you will daily find less and less occasion for your dictionary, as you become more acquainted with the terms; and in the meantime you will read with more satisfaction, because with more understanding. When any point occurs in which you would be glad to have farther information than your book affords you, I beg you would not in the least apprehend that I should think it a trouble to receive and answer your questions. It will be a pleasure, and no trouble. For though I may not be able, out of my own little stock of knowledge, to afford you what you require, I can easily direct you to the books where it may most readily be found.

Adieu, and believe me ever, my dear friend,

B. Franklin

Genius without Education is like Silver in the Mine.

LETTER TO
DR. PRIESTLY

London, September 19, 1772

Dear Sir,

In the affair of so much importance to you, wherein you ask my advice, I cannot, for want of sufficient premises, counsel you what to determine; but, if you please, I will tell you how. When those difficult cases occur, they are difficult chiefly because, while we have them under consideration, all the reasons, pro and con, are not present to the mind at the same time; but sometimes one set present themselves, and at other times another, the first being out of sight. Hence the various purposes or inclinations that alternately prevail, and the uncertainty that perplexes us. To get over this, my way is, to divide half a sheet of paper by a line into two columns, writing over the one pro and over the other con: then, during three or four days' consideration, I put down under the different heads short hints of the different motives that at different times occur to me for or against the measure. When I have thus got them all together in one view, I endeavor to estimate their respective weights, and where I find two (one on each side), that seem equal, I strike them both out. If I find a reason pro equal to some two reasons con I strike out the three. If I judge some two reasons con equal to some three reasons pro, I strike out the five; and, thus proceeding, I find at length where the balance lies; and if, after a day or two of farther consideration, nothing new that is of importance occurs on either side, I come to a determination accordingly. And though the weight of reasons cannot be taken with the precision of algebraic quantities, yet, when each is thus considered separately and comparatively, and the whole lies before me, I think I can judge better, and am less liable to make a rash step; and, in fact, I have found

great advantage from this kind of equation, in what may be called moral or prudential algebra.

Wishing sincerely that you may determine for the best, I am ever, my dear friend, yours most affectionately,

B. Franklin

Wealth is not his that has it, but his that enjoys it.

LETTER TO
BENJAMIN VAUGHAN

Passy, July 10, 1782

By the original law of nations, war and extirpation was the punishment of injury. Humanizing by degrees, it admitted slavery instead of death. A farther step was the exchange of prisoners instead of slavery. Another, to respect more the property of private persons under conquest, and to be content with acquired dominion. Why should not the law of nations go on improving? Ages have intervened between its several steps; but, as knowledge of late increases rapidly, why should not those steps be quickened? Why should it not be agreed to as the future law of nations, that in any war hereafter the following descriptions of men should be undisturbed, have the protection of both sides, and be permitted to follow their employments in surety; viz.,

1. Cultivators of the earth, because they labor for the subsistence of mankind.
2. Fishermen, for the same reason.
3. Merchants and traders in unarmed ships, who accommodate different nations by communicating and exchanging the necessaries and conveniences of life.
4. Artists and mechanics, inhabiting and working in open towns.

It is hardly necessary to add, that the hospitals of enemies should be unmolested; they ought to be assisted.

In short, I would have nobody fought with but those who are paid for fighting. If obliged to take corn from the farmer, friend or enemy, I would pay him for it; the same for the fish or goods of the others.

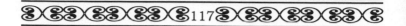

This once established, that encouragement to war which arises from a spirit of rapine would be taken away, and peace, therefore, more likely to continue and be lasting.

B. Franklin

Poverty wants some things,
luxury many things, avarice all things.

LETTER FROM
ANTHONY AFTERWIT

(Note: this was a letter sent to Benjamin Franklin to be published in his paper.)

Mr. Gazetteer, I am an honest tradesman, who never meant harm to anybody. My affairs went on smoothly while a bachelor; but of late I have met with some difficulties, of which I take the freedom to give you an account.

About the time I first addressed my present spouse, her father gave out in speeches that, if she married a man he

liked, he would give with her two hundred pounds in cash on the day of marriage. He never said so much to me, it is true; but he always received me very kindly at his house, and openly countenanced my courtship. I formed several fine schemes what to do with this same two hundred pounds, and in some measure neglected my business on that account; but, unluckily, it came to pass, that, when the old gentleman saw I was pretty well engaged, and that the match was too far gone to be easily broke off, he, without any reason given, grew very angry, forbid me the house, and told his daughter that if she married me he would not give her a farthing. However (as he thought), we were not to be disappointed in that manner, but, having stole a wedding, I took her home to my house, where we were not quite in so poor a condition as the couple described in the Scotch song, who had

> "Neither pot nor pan,
> But four bare legs together,"

for I had a house tolerably well furnished for a poor man before. No thanks to Dad, who, I understand, was very much pleased with his politic management; and I have since learned that there are other old curmudgeons (so called) besides him, who have this trick to marry their daughters, and yet keep what they might well spare till they can keep

it no longer. But this by way of digression; a word to the wise is enough.

I soon saw that with care and industry we might live tolerably easy and in credit with our neighbors; but my wife had a strong inclination to be a gentlewoman. In consequence of this, my old-fashioned looking-glass was one day broke, as she said, no one could tell which way. However, since we could not be without a glass in the room, "My dear," saith she, "we may as well buy a large fashionable one, that Mr. Such-a-one has to sell. It will cost but little more than a common glass, and will look much handsomer and more creditable." Accordingly, the glass was bought and hung against the wall; but in a week's time I was made sensible, by little and little, that the table was by no means suitable to such a glass; and, a more proper table being procured, some time after, my spouse, who was an excellent contriver, informed me where we might have very handsome chairs in the way; and thus, by degrees, I found all my old furniture stowed up in the garret, and everything below altered for the better.

Had we stopped here, it might have done well enough. But my wife being entertained with tea by the good woman she visited, we could do no less than the like when they visited us; so we got a tea table, with all its appurtenances of China and silver. Then my spouse unfortunately

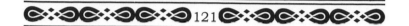

overworked herself in washing the house, so that we could do no longer without a maid. Besides this, it happened frequently that when I came home at one, the dinner was but just put in the pot, and my dear thought really it had been but eleven. At other times, when I came at the same hour, she wondered I would stay so long, for dinner was ready about one, and had waited for me these two hours. These irregularities, occasioned by mistaking the time, convinced me that it was absolutely necessary to buy a clock, which my spouse observed was a great ornament to the room. And lastly, to my grief, she was troubled with some ailment or other, and nothing did her so much good as riding, and these hackney-horses were such wretched ugly creatures that—I bought a very fine pacing mare, which cost twenty pounds; and hereabouts affairs have stood for about a twelvemonth past.

I could see all along that this did not at all suit with my circumstances, but had not resolution enough to help it, till lately, receiving a very severe dun, which mentioned the next court, I began in earnest to project relief. Last Monday, my dear went over the river to see a relation and stay a fortnight, because she could not bear the heat of the town air. In the interim I have taken my turn to make alterations; namely, I have turned away the maid, bag and baggage (for what should we do with a maid, who, besides our boy,

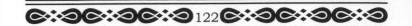

have none but ourselves?) I have sold the pacing mare, and
bought a good milch-cow with three pounds of the money.
I have disposed of the table, and put a good spinning-
wheel in its place, which, methinks, looks very pretty; nine
empty canisters I have stuffed with flax, and with some
of the money of the tea-furniture I have bought a set of
knitting-needles, for, to tell you the truth, I begin to want
stockings. The fine clock I have transformed into an hourglass, by which I have gained a good round sum; and one
of the pieces of the old looking-glass, squared and framed,
supplies the place of the great one, which I have conveyed
into a closet, where it may possibly remain some years. In
short, the face of things is quite changed, and methinks you
would smile to see my hourglass hanging in the place of
the clock. What a great ornament it is to the room! I have
paid my debts, and find money in my pocket. I expect my
dear home next Friday, and, as your paper is taken at the
house where she is, I hope the reading of this will prepare
her mind for the above surprising revolutions. If she
can conform herself to this new manner of living, we
shall be the happiest couple, perhaps, in the province,
and, by the blessing of God, may soon be in thriving
circumstances. I have reserved the great glass, because I
know her heart is set upon it; I will allow her, when she
comes in, to be taken suddenly ill with the headache, the

stomach-ache, fainting-fits, or whatever other disorder she may think more proper, and she may retire to bed as soon as she pleases. But if I should not find her in perfect health, both of body and mind, the next morning, away goes the aforesaid great glass, with several other trinkets I have no occasion for, to the vendue, that very day; which is the irrevocable resolution of, sir, her loving husband and your very humble servant,

Anthony Afterwit

P.S.—I would be glad to know
how you approve my conduct.
Answer. —I don't love to concern
myself in affairs between man and wife.

Wealth and Content are not always Bedfellows.

NOTES

[1] From a letter to Mr. Benjamin Vaughan, dated at Passy, July 26th, 1784. From *Memoirs of Benjamin Franklin; Written by Himself,* 1847.

[2] Truth is brighter than light. From *Memoirs of Benjamin Franklin; Written by Himself,* 1847.

[3] Originally written for the *London Chronicle*, 1776.

[4] A translation of this letter appeared in one of the daily papers of Paris [*Journal de Paris*] about the year 1784. The following is the original piece, with some additions and corrections made in it by the author. From *The Works of Benjamin Franklin, Containing Several Political and Historical Tracts Not Included in any Former Edition, and Many Letters Official and Private Not Hitherto Published*, 1882.

[5] This is one of the author's earliest compositions, it having been written at the beginning of his twenty-third year. It is indeed the first tract of a political nature, which is known to have come from his pen, and although it was published anonymously, yet he afterwards avowed the authorship in his autobiography, where he thus speaks.

"There was a cry among the people for more paper money; only fifteen thousand pounds being extant in the province, and that soon to be sunk. The wealthy inhabitants opposed any addition; being against all paper currency, from the apprehension that it would depreciate as it had done in New England, to the injury of all creditors. We had discussed this point in our junto, where I was on the side of an addition; being persuaded that the first small sum struck in 1723 had done much good by increasing the trade, employment, and number of inhabitants in the province; since I now saw all the old houses inhabited, and many new ones building; whereas I remembered well when I first walked about the streets of Philadelphia, (eating my roll), I saw many of the houses in Walnut Street, between Second and Front Streets, with bills on their doors 'To be let'; and many likewise in Chestnut Street and other streets; which made me think the inhabitants of the city were one after another deserting it. Our debates possessed me so fully on the subject, that I wrote and printed an anonymous pamphlet on it, entitled, 'The Nature and Necessity of a Paper Currency.' It was well received by the common people in general; but the rich men disliked it, for it increased and strengthened the clamor for more money; and, they happening to have no writers among them that were able to answer it, their opposition slackened, and the point was carried by a majority in the House. My friends there, who considered I had been of some service, thought fit to reward me, by employing me in printing the money; a very profitable job, and a great help to me. This was another advantage gained by my being able to write.

"The utility of this currency became, by time and experience, so evident, that the principles upon which it was founded were never afterwards much disputed; so that it grew soon to fifty-five thousand pounds, and in 1739 to eighty thousand pounds, trade, building, and inhabitants all the while increasing. Though I now think there are limits beyond which the quantity may be hurtful."

This enquiry bears the marks of the author's characteristic acuteness and sagacity, but contains some of the fallacies, which were then common in the colonies on the subject of paper money. Occasionally the arguments are addressed more to the popular prejudices, than to the good sense and intelligence of readers, though there is no doubt that Franklin was sincere in supporting the doctrines of the advocates of the paper-money system. He subsequently expressed the same opinions in his examination before the committee of the House of Commons in 1766. This essay is curious, as showing his early impressions, and the rudiments of his thinking upon subjects, which occupied his mind and employed his pen, to a very considerable extent, in the mature period of his life. —Editor. From *The Works of Benjamin Franklin, Containing Several Political and Historical Tracts Not Included in any Former Edition, and Many Letters Official and Private Not Hitherto Published*, 1882.

[6] Some obscurity is thrown over this paragraph by confounding low price with want of demand, and high price with briskness of demand, things which often go together, and which are now, as formerly, often confounded with eachother, though they are by no means identical, one being the cause, the other the effect, respectively; for the increase of demand, out of proportion to that of the supply, increases price, and the reduction of demand, out of proportion to that of supply, reduces price. This inaccuracy, combined with another, which we shall soon meet with in this essay, namely, the confounding of circulating medium, or money, with capital generally; and also another nearly allied to it, namely, the confounding of the amount of capital ready to be loaned, with that of the circulating medium, led to many of the fallacies, which were prevalent

in Franklin's time in subjects of political economy, and which have, to this day, not wholly disappeared from similar speculations. The propositions really in question in this part of the essay are, that briskness of trade promotes production and consequently wealth, and that plenty, or rather a sufficiency, of circulating medium promotes trade, and a want of it, on the other hand, obstructs trade. These propositions are sufficiently plain, and are indisputable, and they constitute the author's premises or postulates, but they will not be found to lead to all his conclusions. — W. Phillips. From *The Works of Benjamin Franklin, Containing Several Political and Historical Tracts Not Included in any Former Edition, and Many Letters Official and Private Not Thitherto Published*, 1882.

[7] This proposition is true, and yet it tends to leave a wrong impression on the mind; for money, like ships, is an instrument of trade, and, like ploughs, is an instrument of production, and the more facilities for trade and production, and consequently for obtaining wealth, the country afforded, the greater were the inducements to emigrate to it. The quality of the ships, and ploughs, &c., is as important as the number. Just so of the circulating medium; the soundness of the currency is quite as important as its abundance. The error left upon the mind by the above language, and it is a very common one, is, that there is some predominant and almost magical effect belonging to a circulating medium,

as distinguished from other instruments and facilities of production and trade, and their result, wealth; whereas the quantity of even a sound currency is not decisive of the prosperity of a country, as might be seen in Franklin's time in some of the South American provinces. —W. Phillips. From *The Works of Benjamin Franklin, Containing Several Political and Historical Tracts Not Included in any Former Edition, and Many Letters Official and Private Not Hitherto Published*, 1882.

[8] Franklin states this doctrine in 1729, precisely as Adam Smith does forty-six years afterwards in The Wealth of Nations. —W. Phillips. From *The Works of Benjamin Franklin, Containing Several Political and Historical Tracts Not Included in any Former Edition, and Many Letters Official and Private Not Hitherto Published*, 1882.

[9] This passage shows that the theory, as to the effect of the South American mines upon the rate of money prices and the reduction of the value of the precious metals, so elaborately set forth and reasoned out by Adam Smith, was quite a familiar notion when he was but six years old; the correctness of which, however, to the extent laid down by Franklin in this place, and afterwards by Smith, has of late years been gravely questioned by very respectable writers. —W. Phillips. From *The Works of Benjamin Franklin, Containing Several Political and Historical Tracts Not Included in any Former Edition, and Many Letters Official and Private Not Hitherto Published*, 1882.

[10] This is a clear and just view of the effects and utility of banks of deposit. But the application, which Franklin is about to make of it to land banks, will not be acquiesced in at this day. Everybody knows, that certainty as to time of payment of bills, that pass as a circulating medium, is no less important than the certainty that they will be eventually paid. The convertibility of the fund pledged for the redemption of the bills is as material a circumstance as its sufficiency and permanency of value. Land, and immovable property generally, is less convertible than movable property, for it cannot be removed from its place to seek a market; this renders this kind of property peculiarly unfit to constitute a fund or pledge for the redemption of bills that circulate as money. —W Phillips. From *The Works of Benjamin Franklin, Containing Several Political and Historical Tracts Not Included in any Former Edition, and Many Letters Official and Private Not Hitherto Published*, 1882.

[11] All commerce is by exchange, or rather is exchange, whether a trade involves money or not. The kind of trade intended by the author is in technical as well as in common language known by the name of barter. — W. Phillips. From *The Works of Benjamin Franklin, Containing Several Political and Historical Tracts Not Included in any Former Edition, and Many Letters Official and Private Not Thitherto Published*, 1882

[12] Here is the error mentioned in a previous note; the author confounds circulating medium with loanable capital.

Thus, by the common phrase scarcity of money, we always mean scarcity of money or capital to be loaned, which is quite a different thing from insufficiency of the quantity of the circulating medium for the purposes of trade. The two may be contemporaneous, but they are different things. It may readily be imagined that trade, and production, and investments generally, may be so profitable, that people would prefer to invest or employ their capital themselves, rather than loan it to others to be invested or employed. This state of things has no necessary connexion with the sufficiency of the quantity of circulating medium. Money in this sense may be plenty, when in the other it is scarce. This is a state of things, which does in fact often happen —W. Phillips. From *The Works of Benjamin Franklin, Containing Several Political and Historical Tracts Not Included in any Former Edition, and Many Letters Official and Private Not Hitherto Published*, 1882.

[13] This passage is obscure, a fault with which Franklin's writings are rarely chargeable. It is so far from being true that no man in his senses will mortgage his land for what is of no more value to him than that which he mortgages, that it is the most common practice to mortgage lands and personal property for what is not of half the value of either. The lender often demands security exceeding the value loaned. Perhaps the meaning is, that the money must be of more convenience or use to the borrower than

the land mortgaged for it, or he would not borrow; and that it could not be of such convenience and use to him if an excess had been issued, whereby its value and utility would be diminished. —W. Phillips. From *The Works of Benjamin Franklin, Containing Several Political and Historical Tracts Not Included in any Former Edition, and Many Letters Official and Private Not Hitherto Published*, 1882.

[14] But there was another view of the case presented by the opposers of paper currency, which Franklin omits. If a man has mortgaged his land for a hundred pounds, and invested the money in the purchase of other land, and two years afterwards, when the money has depreciated in value fifty percent, sells half of the land he purchased for a hundred pounds and pays off his debt, though the land may not have risen at all in the meantime, he makes a very good operation, at the expense of those through whose hands the money has been passing in the meantime. This was the operation of the paper-money system to which the opposers of that system objected. —W. Phillips. From *The Works of Benjamin Franklin, Containing Several Political and Historical Tracts Not Included in any Former Edition, and Many Letters Official and Private Not Hitherto Published*, 1882.

[15] The author passes this objection with a very slight consideration, and on the whole rather disingenuously and like a partisan, as he and every other man in the province were, at the time, on one side or the other of the question. He had

immediately before said, that, in case of excess, the surplus would be returned, and of course there could not be a lasting excess if this was the case. But here he supposes there may be a surplus until the increase of business shall absorb it, and that such increase will be sufficient for the purpose. Now the first supposition is palpably not well founded, in regard to a money redeemable at some future day, as was the provincial paper money generally. As to the second supposition, that any quantity of such paper that can be issued, will be used and eventually needed, there are abundant examples to the contrary. —W. Phillips. From *The Works of Benjamin Franklin, Containing Several Political and Historical Tracts Not Included in any Former Edition, and Many Letters Official and Private Not Hitherto Published*, 1882.

[16] Soon after this pamphlet was written, the measure proposed in it was adopted by the Assembly of Pennsylvania; and subsequently another bill for a similar object was passed, the principal features of which were published by Governor Pownall. They were understood to have been communicated to him by Franklin, with other remarks on paper money. The proceedings of the Assembly on the subject are described in the extract below.

"As the paper-money act made and passed in Pennsylvania, in 1739, was the completest of the kind, containing all the improvements which experience had from time to time suggested, in the execution of preceding acts; an account of that act will best explain and recommend the measure contained in the following proposal.

"The sum of the notes, by that act directed to be printed, was eighty thousand pounds proclamation money. This money was to be emitted to the several borrowers, from a loan-office established for that purpose.

"Five persons were nominated trustees of the loan-office, under whose care and direction, the bills or notes were to be printed and emitted.

"To suit the bills for a common currency, they were of small and various denominations, from twenty shillings downwards to one shilling.

"Various precautions were taken, to prevent counterfeits, by peculiarities in the paper, character, manner of printing, signing, numbering, &c.

"The trustees took an oath, and gave security for the due and faithful execution of their office.

"They were to lend out the bills on real security of at least double the value, for a term of sixteen years, to be repaid in yearly quotas or installments, with interest. Thus one sixteenth part of the principal was yearly paid back into the office, which made the payment easy to the borrower. This interest was applied to public services, the principal, during the first ten years, let out again to fresh borrowers.

"The new borrowers, from year to year, were to have the money only for the remaining part of the term of sixteen years, repaying, by fewer and, of course, proportionably larger installments, and during the last six years of the sixteen, the sums paid in were not to be remitted, but the notes burnt and destroyed; so that, at the end of the sixteen years, the whole might be called in and burnt, and the accounts completely settled." From *The Works of Benjamin Franklin, Containing Several Political and Historical Tracts Not Included in any Former Edition, and Many Letters Official and Private Not Hitherto Published*, 1882.